Out of the Canyon

Out of the Canyon

Retracing New Steps Home
amidst Human Suffering

Jeffrey C. Tucker

RESOURCE *Publications* • Eugene, Oregon

OUT OF THE CANYON
Retracing New Steps Home amidst Human Suffering

Copyright © 2016 Jeffrey C. Tucker. All rights reserved. Except for brief quotations in critical publications or reviews, no part of this book may be reproduced in any manner without prior written permission from the publisher. Write: Permissions, Wipf and Stock Publishers, 199 W. 8th Ave., Suite 3, Eugene, OR 97401.

Resource Publications
An Imprint of Wipf and Stock Publishers
199 W. 8th Ave., Suite 3
Eugene, OR 97401

www.wipfandstock.com

PAPERBACK ISBN: 978-1-5326-0526-0
HARDCOVER ISBN: 978-1-5326-0528-4
EBOOK ISBN: 978-1-5326-0527-7

Manufactured in the U.S.A.   NOVEMBER 21, 2016

Dedication

"If I ever become a Saint—I will surely be one of 'darkness'. I will continually be absent from Heaven—to light the light of those in darkness on earth."

MOTHER TERESA

THIS BOOK IS DEDICATED to those who have blindly crawled the shadowy canyon trail of human suffering; who have pushed onward in spite of pain and loss; and who have lit the path of light and love for those who follow.

Contents

Foreword | xi
Introduction | xv

Canyon Trail Leg One: Biblical Voices of Suffering
Leg One Canyon Trail Preview | 3
Trail Log: Day 1–The Suffering of Separation | 5
Trail Log: Day 2–The Suffering of Forsakenness | 6
Trail Log: Day 3–The Suffering of Lost Purpose | 7
Trail Log: Day 4–The Suffering of Lost Identity | 8
Trail Log: Day 5–The Suffering of Lost Control | 9
Trail Log: Day 6–The Suffering of Fear | 10
Trail Log: Day 7–The Suffering of Persecution | 11
Trail Log: Day 8–The Problem with the Biblical Voices | 12
Trail Log: Day 9–Listening to God's Voice | 13
Final Thoughts for This Leg | 14

Canyon Trail Leg Two: The Problem with our Suffering Voices
Leg Two Canyon Trail Preview | 17
Trail Log: Day 10–Lack of Feeling Vocabulary | 18
Trail Log: Day 11–Lack of Active Listening | 19
Trail Log: Day 12–Lack of Real Communication | 20
Trail Log: Day 13–Lack of Trust | 21
Trail Log: Day 14–Lack of Urgency | 22
Trail Log: Day 15–Lack of Individuality | 23
Trail Log: Day 16–Lack of Coping | 24
Trail Log: Day 17–Lack of Any Feeling | 25
Trail Log: Day 18–Lack of Curiosity | 26
Trail Log: Day 19–Lack of God | 27
Final Thoughts for This Leg | 28

Canyon Trail Leg Three: The Roots of the Problem
Leg Three Canyon Trail Preview | 31

Contents

Trail Log: Day 20–My Transference to God | 32
Trail Log: Day 21–God Versus Chaos | 33
Trail Log: Day 22–Life Versus Death: Part One | 34
Trail Log: Day 23–Life Versus Death: Part Two | 35
Trail Log: Day 24–Prayers to God | 36
Trail Log: Day 25–Unholy Alliance | 37
Trail Log: Day 26–Thing Versus Whole Person | 38
Trail Log: Day 27–Control Versus Freedom | 39
Trail Log: Day 28–Unconscious Versus Conscious | 40
Trail Log: Day 29–Lost Translation | 41
Trail Log: Day 30–Unconscious Origins | 42
Trail Log: Day 31–Mid-Life | 43
Trail Log: Day 32–Anger Versus Hurt | 44
Trail Log: Day 33–Becoming a Victim | 45
Trail Log: Day 34–Brokenness | 46
Trail Log: Day 35–Courage Rather Than Fear | 47
Final Thoughts for This Leg | 48

Canyon Trail Leg Four: Our God Problem: Theodicy
Leg Four Canyon Trail Preview | 51
Trail Log: Day 36–Three-in-One | 52
Trail Log: Day 37–Hiding Behind God | 53
Trail Log: Day 38–Good and Evil | 54
Trail Log: Day 39–Blaming God | 55
Trail Log: Day 40–Ambivalent Feelings Towards God | 56
Trail Log: Day 41–The Human Trinity: Part One | 57
Trail Log: Day 42–The Human Trinity: Part Two | 58
Trail Log: Day 43–The Human Trinity: Part Three | 59
Trail Log: Day 44–Rethinking Theodicy and God | 60
Final Thoughts for This Leg | 61

Canyon Trail Leg Five: Violent and Traumatic Suffering
Leg Five Canyon Trail Preview | 65
Trail Log: Day 45–Connections Unconnected | 66
Trail Log: Day 46–The Violence of Violence | 67
Trail Log: Day 47–The Victims are Victimized | 68
Trail Log: Day 48–The Prisoner Lens | 69
Trail Log: Day 49–The Lens of Trauma | 70
Trail Log: Day 50–Processing Violence and Trauma | 71
Trail Log: Day 51–A Mother God | 72
Trail Log: Day 52–God in Trauma and Violence | 73

CONTENTS

Final Thoughts for This Leg | 74

Canyon Trail Leg Six: Supporting the Longer-Term Needs of Suffering: Spirituality
Leg Six Canyon Trail Preview | 77
Trail Log: Day 53–Spirituality Defined | 78
Trail Log: Day 54–The Trap of Religiosity | 79
Trail Log: Day 55–The Spiritual Whole: Part One | 80
Trail Log: Day 56–The Spiritual Whole: Part Two | 81
Trail Log: Day 57–The Spiritual Whole: Part Three | 82
Trail Log: Day 58–Levels of Spirituality | 83
Trail Log: Day 59–Spiritual Practices: The Sacred One | 84
Trail Log: Day 60–Spiritual Practices: Creation | 85
Trail Log: Day 61–Spiritual Practices: Belonging | 86
Trail Log: Day 62–Spiritual Practices: Silence | 87
Trail Log: Day 63–Spiritual Practices: Simplicity | 88
Trail Log: Day 64–Spiritual Practices: Honor | 89
Trail Log: Day 65–Spiritual Practices: Seasons of Life | 90
Final Thoughts for This Leg | 91

Canyon Trail Leg Seven: Supporting the Immediate Needs of Suffering
Leg Seven Canyon Trail Preview | 95
Trail Log: Day 66–Coping Pitfalls: Maladaptive Ones | 96
Trail Log: Day 67–Coping Pitfalls: Keep It Running | 97
Trail Log: Day 68–Coping Pitfalls: My Decision-Making | 98
Trail Log: Day 69–Coping Pitfalls: Mangled Bicycle Wheel | 99
Trail Log: Day 70–The Intersection of Coping | 100
Trail Log: Day 71–Coping—Another Way: Information | 101
Trail Log: Day 72–Coping—Another Way: Linkages | 102
Trail Log: Day 73–Coping—Another Way: Keeping Me in Touch | 103
Trail Log: Day 74–Coping—Another Way: Keep it Simple | 104
Trail Log: Day 75–Coping—Another Way: Find a Friend | 105
Final Thoughts for This Leg | 106

Canyon Trail Leg Eight: The Path of Healing and Transformation
Leg Eight Canyon Trail Preview | 109
Trail Log: Day 76–Creating a New Story | 110
Trail Log: Day 77–Movement Forward | 111
Trail Log: Day 78–Reflection on my Actions | 112
Trail Log: Day 79–Incorporation without Refreezing | 113
Trail Log: Day 80–Becoming More 'Whole' | 114
Trail Log: Day 81–Becoming 'Healthier' | 115

CONTENTS

Trail Log: Day 82–Becoming More Creative | 116
Trail Log: Day 83–Becoming More Forgiving | 117
Trail Log: Day 84–Becoming More Integral | 118
Trail Log: Day 85–Becoming More Generous | 119
Trail Log: Day 86–Becoming More God-Filled | 120
Final Thoughts for This Leg | 121

Canyon Trail Leg Nine: When We Don't 'Heal'
Leg Nine Canyon Trail Preview | 125
Trail Log: Day 87–Just Got the News | 126
Trail Log: Day 88–Taking Stock: So Now What? | 127
Trail Log: Day 89–Taking Stock: What's Still Possible? | 128
Trail Log: Day 90–Taking Stock: Of My Hope | 129
Trail Log: Day 91–Taking Stock: Wishes and Fears | 130
Trail Log: Day 92–Taking Stock: Blessings and Losses | 131
Trail Log: Day 93–Taking Stock: Of My Past | 132
Trail Log: Day 94–Taking Stock: Of My Feelings About God | 133
Trail Log: Day 95–Taking Stock: Letting Go | 134
Trail Log: Day 96–Taking Stock: Letting God | 135
Final Thoughts for This Leg | 136

Canyon Trail Leg Ten: What We Need in Caregivers
Leg Ten Canyon Trail Preview | 139
Trail Log: Day 97–Barriers to Caring: Systems Based | 140
Trail Log: Day 98–Barriers to Caring: Individually Based | 141
Trail Log: Day 99–Barriers to Caring: Ownership Based | 142
Trail Log: Day 100–Barriers to Caring: Distance Based | 143
Trail Log: Day 101–Barriers to Caring: Worldview Based | 144
Trail Log: Day 102–The Role of the Caregiver | 145
Trail Log: Day 103–What the Role Implies | 146
Trail Log: Day 104–Into the Chaos | 147
Final Thoughts for This Leg | 148

Final Thoughts from the Trail | 149

Things That I Need to Think Even More About | 151
Postscript | 153
With Infinite Gratitude | 157

Foreword

IN MY PREVIOUS BOOK, *The End of the Island*, I wrote an engaging and accessible theology of human suffering. This second book in the series begins where *The End of the Island* left off—but this time with a different story and a focus on the behavioral and pastoral care side of things. Before we move forward together, though, it's important to get re-grounded in the theology from which I write. For it will broadly frame the ideas and guidance in the pages that will follow.

Theology is a shared human dialogue about God. It is grounded in a basic faith, but it also seeks greater understanding, clarity, and articulation. This understanding is informed by Biblical reference, tradition, logic, and experience. They all matter, guide, and inform. I read the Bible daily, and I view it as one primary source. But God continues to speak, I believe. Theology is, therefore, most useful when it is based primarily on our *experience* with God. Our life in faith is that which we each experience in unique and profound ways. In the realm of this experience, I also propose that our respective contexts matter much. The experiences of the poor, sick and suffering, and marginalized differ significantly from those of persons with far greater resources, privilege, opportunity, and physical health. As such, how we think and talk about God is grounded by our own time, contexts, situations, and perceived identities. We do not think about theology as much as we experience and live it—through God's presence, transformation, and being: God's life and actions in our own lives past, present, and future.

I believe that God is the source of all creation and of all life. Therefore, God is a God of life in all its fullness and abundance. Creation, itself, embodies God's unmerited love. Second, life in its fullness implies not just creative love, but also justice. God has created us to live as inherently loved and worthy individuals in communities of interdependency and fairness. Third, God is a God of liberation. Fullness and abundance mean human freedom from dehumanization, marginalization, discrimination, and hatred. Lastly, God is present. God did not simply create and walk away. God is present in history and in our lives now in order to work in ways that help to model life, love, justice, liberation, and transformation. God is present with all. However, I believe that God is present in special, more profound, transformational, and sustaining ways to and with the poor, sick, marginalized, and rejected. Not because they are more worthy, without sin, or blameless. But because of this: If God loves the fullness of life, justice, and liberation, it actually pains God when some thrive at the expense of those who are 'other', victimized, and left out.

The world that God created is not static. It operates as a free, dynamic, evolving, fluid, and sometimes messy enterprise. Our 'living room' on this planet can be cluttered, chaotic, and dysfunctional. The china, crystal, and even the furniture all experience breakage. So do we as humans. We are finite, mortal, and evolving beings in God. Brokenness is therefore an inherent part of our world, our lives, and our environment. However, I view brokenness not so much as sinfulness, per se, but instead as representing the forces, decisions, setbacks, and randomness in life that inhibit the God-given spirituality in us.

Spirituality is based on our born, inherent connectedness with God, each other, our environment, our meaning and purpose, our unique gifts, and the light of love that God has placed in each of us at conception. When that inherent Spirituality is eroded, rejected, neglected, or clouded by individual or institutional decisions, addictions, relationships, rejection, or even the negative randomness in life, we become less human. Our connectedness with God, with ourselves, and with others begins to fray. First at the edges, then throughout. Inasmuch as God has given us human freedom, we are accountable for our own part in this 'tearing apart'. However, I do not believe that we are inherently sinful or that we are bequeathed this sinfulness as a result of our lineage with Adam and Eve. Instead, we are born into a world that often works against our Spiritual Wholeness. This is not God's plan. We were given birth by God in order to journey toward this wholeness. We have the tools already placed within us by God. But sometimes, we must 'swim against the current' in the face of life's inevitable brokenness.

If human brokenness is an inevitable part of our lives, we are healed and transformed in the context of those very same lives. In my own Christian faith tradition, we believe that Jesus Christ is the primary author of our salvation. We also often say that Christ's atoning death makes that salvation possible. However, I would respectfully beg to differ. If God is a God of life, God did not condemn Christ to die on the Cross. God is not a child abuser and killer in the name of cleansing our sins. *We* killed Jesus. And God cried this loss of life. God grieved this death. We are, therefore, not saved by Christ's death, but by the entirety of Christ's being. Further, Christ was not simply divine. He was also human. He was born into poverty, lived as a homeless person, was rejected for his lineage as a Galilean, and was scorned for his 'otherness' as a prophet. He worked, healed, ministered, and lived. Christ embodied God's plan for us through the entirety of his incarnation, work, actions, and proclamation of God's Reign (plan). While that Reign is future to an extent, Christ actually 'lived' it while here on earth.

Christians believe that Christ died and then rose. His rising tells me powerfully that God's plan and love win. Life triumphs over death. Love triumphs over hatred, even hatred against God in God's name. Hope triumphs over despair. Death, hatred, and despair can and are transformed by a God who wants life for all of us: Life as God intended. As such, I hold that Christ's resurrection is not simply some individualized, personal life raft to eternity. 'Resurrection' also means our life lived right here and now. Life is a participatory (and sometimes even a contact) sport. Life must be lived in all of its messiness and sorrow. Life is lived in Spiritual, whole ways that God can actually use and redeem for the future Reign in all its fullness.

In the context of truly being and living, we heal by our openness to the future. We heal through our trust in a God who wants to be present to and in us. We heal through a God who sits with us; walks with us; weeps for us; carries us when we can no longer walk ourselves; and who loves us even when we no longer do so. We heal through a God who 'heals' us in transformational ways, even when these ways do not appear to 'cure' us. Even when we don't get 'better' in the eyes of others. We heal through a God who connects us with others and with help, when we need it most. We heal through a God who opens possibilities, keeps hope alive, and comforts when those hopes appear to dim. We heal through a God who holds us in the palms of God's hands, when no other hands reach out for us. We heal when we create space for God to enter into us and keep the pilot light of our very being and soul burning, even if we won't or couldn't 'make it'. We heal when we let God give meaning and purpose to our life, even if it isn't life as we had imagined it.

Healing takes active faith and trust that God cares, grieves, and transforms even the most difficult and hopeless situations. Even situations of poverty, sickness, rejection, injustice, and 'otherness' in the eyes of others. As a chaplain, I humbly come alongside this process. I am a fellow traveler who meets patients, families, and staff right where they are—feeling with, not feeling sorry for. I strive to compassionately and less anxiously enter into their suffering in ways that facilitate their discovery or re-discovery of their identity as loved and inherently valuable persons. In so doing, I work to support their self-empowered reflection and insights; their naming and expressing of their feelings; their meaning-making; their connections with others; and their hope as affirmed, loved persons, even in the face of their pain and loss. This, I believe, honors God's plan for us: Life lived abundantly and in all its fullness. Life lived in love and in communion, no matter what life brings our way.

Foreword

Each of us can also 'chaplain' others in their pain and loss, whether we know it or not. We do so when we gently enter into the suffering of another, grounded in love, respect, affirmation, and active listening. Whether the other person is dying, homeless, suffers addiction, is hungry, has been abused or neglected, lives with AIDS or cancer, or has just lost their child to a sudden death, we can sit with and remain in the pain of another. As much as we may want to flee, we can stay. We cannot take away the pain of another in the process, but we can remain with it. We can share it with another for a moment. In so doing, we can share our very own wounded, but loved, selves. Together, we can embrace the great mystery of death and suffering, while knowing that God has a plan that transcends even the most hopeless situation. In God's time and place. We can accept the uncertainties and losses with faith. Simultaneously, we can embrace God's plan with joyful hope. And something truly amazing can, therefore, happen along the way. We can *both* be healed in the process. Together. That's the way God intended from the very start.

Introduction

HUMAN SUFFERING CAN FEEL like an unexpected trip to the Emergency Department of a hospital. It's as if everything was going well, until it wasn't after all. The day started normally, like any other day. A good, promising day, actually. Until everything went suddenly wrong. Totally and completely so. Things were moving along nicely, even smoothly. A nice, easy ride. Until the speed bumps approached, absolutely unnoticed. Until a large pothole in the road swallowed my car. And me. It was the best day in my life. Well maybe not the best, but a very good one, to be sure. Until it became the worst one that I've ever lived thus far. Everything was looking shiny, bright, and unblemished. Until it all crashed. And was totaled. Completely crumpled and mangled. Towed away. Not even a chance to say goodbye. Suddenly, everything changed. . . forever.

The Emergency Department is an apt metaphor for human suffering. For it represents the clinical starkness of the ugly changes created by our sudden pain and loss. Walk around Emergency and you'll see periods of quiet and seeming boredom punctuated by spurts of frenetic activity. These spikes come with little warning. "Trauma Alert – E.T.A. in 5 minutes." Casual conversations about daily life, families, vacation plans, weekend debriefs, and sundry other topics abruptly stop. Fixed eyes turn from computer screens. Paperwork is left sitting in place. Everyone moves quickly. It's time for fight or flight. Except it's a false choice. There is no flight. There's only fight. There's only response. And Now.

Picture yourself rolling into a hospital Emergency Department Trauma Bay as a patient. Injured. In pain. Suffering traumatically. Everyone is waiting for you. A lot of people. The doors swing open and the transporting paramedic immediately begins his or her briefing to the Trauma staff. All listen intently. The dialogue is crisp, clinical, and matter-of fact. Data. Vitals. Then, questions for you, as the patient, from the staff. Clinical. Crisp. Matter-of-fact. "What happened? Where? Can you move this? Turn your head this way." Then, your clothes are cut off of you. Like a buzz cut instead of a styling. So much for your privacy and even your dignity. You're now being acted upon.

IVs are placed in you. Blood is taken. Then you're off for a CT Scan. Quickly. You see monitors and lines. Bright lights shine in your face. You might

Introduction

be on camera. You're being handled by people in plastic gowns and gloves. They look almost unreal. And the sounds that surround you are surreal. Not like your favorite song. Not like the soft and gentle breeze that you hear on a warm summer day. There's no rhythm to the beat, I'm afraid. Beeps here. High pitch sounds there. Voices everywhere. Overheads are blaring as you move from room to room. There is no silence here. As you leave the Trauma Bay, you pass rows of open cubicles. Short walls separate the staff across from them. A cold separation in the midst of a crowd of people. You'll hear persons talking about you as 'the patient in Room 3'. Somehow, you just lost your name and your identity. You were Bill Wilson until this all started. Now you're Room 3. And while you're waiting between interventions, you hear others outside your room. They're talking, conversing, and comparing notes. Life seems to be marching on for them. But wait a minute. "I'm in pain here. I thought the world stopped for me." News flash: It didn't. Life is cruising forward. For the moment without you.

You're on the clock. You're being charted and documented and monitored to the hilt. You're confronted with a bunch of strangers you've never met before. They try to talk in your language, but you don't understand a lot of what's going on. They ask you what you think, what you want to do, whether you've completed any advance directives for end-of-life care. One minute, you're hearing from one specialist. The next minute, from another. Everyone's a specialist here. Yes, and they all want to know how you 'feel'. But it's mostly about where it hurts most. 1-10. On a scale. Body pain. In your head. On your arms or legs. In your abdomen. In your chest. What's your oxygen level? Blood pressure measures. Temperature. Scan or test results.

But how are you really feeling? Not numbers or symptoms. Not test results or pain levels. Rather, how are you feeling *about* all of this? About the fact that your life just became a train wreck one hour ago. Like the fact that you're scared out of your living wits at the moment. Like the fact that you feel utterly alone, disempowered, disembodied, and unsure whether you'll ever leave this place. At least alive. Did anyone get the memo today? "I Am Suffering Inside." Inside my soul. Inside my being. There are no measures or tests for that. I simply feel it in my gut. In my heart. Not in my bodily organs or bodily functions. In me. In the world that was just fine earlier in the day. Until everything got traumatically upended. When my routine, my meaning, my relationships, my work, my purpose, and my passions got violently overturned. Until the status quo was irrevocably shaken by a tornado-like fluidity and change coming down on me. Like a hurricane-force avalanche of mud, ice, and snow. And here lies me. In the mud, ice, and snow.

Introduction

In your moment of human suffering, you may be only *figuratively* in a hospital Emergency Department. But it probably feels like it to you. Or worse. Perhaps you feel as if you've been abandoned in a vacant field somewhere. Or on the battlefield. Or, better yet, within a deep, wide, barren, and foreboding canyon. Not clinical-looking and antiseptic-feeling like a hospital. Instead, breathing and walking within the grit, dirt, sweat, and chills of being directly outside. In *all* of the elements. Not even a room number here. For everyone's in the same room at the bottom of the canyon. And, in the canyon of your suffering, you come face-to-face with your own mortality—perhaps for the very first time. In your suffering, pain, and loss, you confront our most haunting existential reality: your own finiteness as a person. And of all those that you love or care about. Each of us is born with an abiding sense of our own mortality. The very act of our beginning sets in motion our ultimate end. We are born. We live. Then we die. No way out of that one. Scary, in fact. In fact, so scary a proposition that we don't much talk about it. "Let's change the subject and talk about something more pleasant. Pass the potatoes, please."

Until the subject forcibly changes on us, and you're confronted with it. In the Trauma Bay. In the hospital. On the battlefield. Or within a dark, gigantic, and dangerous canyon. Maybe *your* canyon is a friend's funeral. Or spending your first holiday alone after the death of a loved one. Or hearing a grim diagnosis for your health. Or losing your livelihood. Or your home. But what if all that you most fear in your suffering revolves around this: you are scared to death about death itself. Death is the thing that awaits us all in the end. The randomness of it all. The unfairness of it all. The darkness of it all. The starkness of it all. So you try to change the subject. But most of all, you try to control it all. If only you can somehow manage the inherent chaos around you, you'll cut it off. You'll find a way. You'll outsmart it. You'll buy more lives. Like a cat. And, in the process, you manage, plan, forestall, scheme, deny, deflect, and flee. All in the name of keeping your end at bay. Or all in the name of chaos control. The status quo. Keep the good times rolling. Pass the potatoes and change the subject.

In the pages ahead, I'll endeavor to meet the realities of life, suffering, and death right where they sit. I'll courageously hit them head-on, thank you, without changing the subject. And I'll try to stay on topic. Having said that, I offer you, the reader, not a grim resignation to our indelible human fate in the pages ahead. Quite to the contrary. I'll accept our human finiteness and suffering as a journey *Out of the Canyon*. I'll use a broad and deep canyon as my analogy for what it's like to walk in and through suffering. I'll offer you not an escape from life and death—from the canyon—but, instead, a trail guide for living with more peace, progress, and joyfulness within this space. Within the canyon, itself. On the First Leg of our trek, we'll explore the many Biblical voices of suffering. Even God's people were not spared this reality. On the Second Leg, we'll talk about the problems with our own suffering voices. Specifically the things we say and do that muffle our speech; what we most often listen for; the things that exacerbate our pain and loss; and the false choices that we often try to make. On the Third Leg of our journey out of the canyon, we'll search for the roots of our suffering, pain, and loss. We'll look at the many dynamic and often conflicting forces that help to create, maintain, and exacerbate our problems. On the Fourth Leg, we'll discuss God's place in our suffering. More specifically, the problem with Theodicy: The notion that God is good, just, fair, and loving. Yet we still suffer. In so doing, I'll offer another, potentially healthier way to look at God's power and presence in the midst of our suffering.

Our Fifth Leg will feature a look at violent and traumatic suffering. Specifically, how this type of suffering differs from others in its form and its impact on us when we experience it. On the Sixth Leg, we'll explore Spirituality as the primary foundation in supporting the longer-term needs of human suffering. I'll discuss how this differs from religiosity, and offer a number of ideas and disciplines that can help us to become more 'whole'—even in the face of our pain and loss. On the Seventh Leg of our trek, we'll explore how we can support the more immediate needs of suffering. I'll discuss our often maladaptive coping mechanisms, and why they don't work. Conversely, I'll offer simple, helpful, and practical tools that can accompany us as we enter into our own suffering.

On the Eighth Leg of our canyon journey, we'll explore the path of healing and transformation. I'll offer ways in which we can more successfully address the changes that suffering bring to our lives. Ways in which we can use even our pain to become stronger, more flexible, and more whole. On the Ninth Leg, I'll acknowledge that sometimes we (and those whom we love) don't heal as we often define it. I'll offer an alternative definition of the word 'healing'. I'll inquire into what is still possible when we can no longer heal clinically. Miracles of living come in many different packages. One size does not fit all. In the Tenth and Final Leg, I'll offer practical guidance on how each of us can become better, more compassionate, and helpful caregivers. I'll discuss the multi-faceted role of caregivers and what that role entails. I'll talk about barriers to empathy. I'll discuss how the qualities that we already have, or can iteratively cultivate, can effectively break these barriers down. I'll look squarely at what we can bring into the space of suffering chaos: Our own pain or that of another.

Out of the Canyon is not an easy book to travel the path of suffering with. Then again, suffering, loss, and pain aren't easy either. I promise you this, though. If you'll put on your boots, tie up your laces, and strap on your backpack, we'll head out together now. You'll never travel alone. I'll write in accessible ways that make this journey together more digestible, possible, and

Introduction

promising. I'll write honestly, but not morosely. I'll talk a little behavioral and pastoral care theory, but I'll also offer something quite practical, engaging, and usable for each of you while we're on the path. I'll even use some humor along the way. For we meet our human suffering not just with our tears and our grit and our sweat. We meet it *also* with our smiles, our laughter, and our joyful stories of yet another healing milestone actually met today. Finally, I'll write from the broad context of a Christian seminary graduate and one who practices a Christian faith tradition. However, I'll write to you far more as an inclusive and interdenominational chaplain and author. For pain, loss, and suffering know no single religion, no single practice, and no single face. I'll, therefore, try to meet you wherever *you* are in your own journey. I respect and honor the diverse faith traditions of humanity. And I'll do my best to speak to you all in your rich diversity. All are welcome. So let's get started, shall we? Out of the Canyon. Together...

Canyon Trail Leg One:
Biblical Voices of Suffering

"My God, my God, why have you forsaken me? Why are you so far from helping me, from the words of my groaning? O my God, I cry by day, but you do not answer; and by night, but find no rest."

PSALM 22: 1–2

Leg One Canyon Trail Preview

So... God. Are you actually listening? How did I end up here? Everything was going just fine with my life. Or so I thought. I have a lot of emotional scars from my growing up years. And more from my later years, I guess. I never properly grieved the many losses, as it turns out. I never surfaced the pain, as it turned in. It was there, to be sure. But I hadn't dealt with it. And I've paid dearly for it. Here I am now in the latter portion of my life. And I'm finally facing it all. After so many years. Those intervening years don't make it any easier. In fact, they make it tougher. For the pain has calcified on me. Got hardened into my veins and arteries. I'm older now. And so are my hardened veins and arteries. But I've decided to acknowledge my suffering, nonetheless. To name it. To enter into it and experience it. No matter what. But in order to do that, I need to walk through the canyon. The canyon of my suffering. Of my pain. Of my losses. The canyon that was hidden away from me for so many years. Now it's out in the open and it's staring menacingly at me. The canyon...

So I'm just about to walk into this canyon, God. The canyon is the only way, I'm afraid. I need to enter it, walk it, finish it, and walk out of it. Then, all the bad stuff will end, right? I've been looking at my canyon trail guide—the map of this enormous place. And the map says that the canyon trail has many legs. With many trials. With some risk. And some more pain along the way. I'm too tired to ask how I got here in the first place. It doesn't matter really. I simply need to enter into *this* place. The canyon. So, I take my first steps on the first leg of the journey in... and out.

According to the trail map, the first leg is a challenging one. The path is narrow. And it says here that I shouldn't leave the trail. Not even a little bit. Ever. For if I do, I'll get stuck. In the mud. Right off the path. Or I'll get lost. Or get caught in the prickly vines that border the trail. Or in the thick undergrowth. Or in the poison ivy. Just thinking about it makes me itch. So, I need to stay on the path. That's what it says. But what if there's a better way? Even *another* way. Is it possible that the well-worn path isn't the only way? I pray that you'll guide me, whatever the way, God. Help me to stay on the path, but listen to it with open eyes. With curiosity. With questions. Let me speak my doubts to you. Tell me if you want me to take another way at times along the way. For, surely, there isn't only one way. For, in the end, aren't *You* the way, God? Keep me listening, Lord. Please. Thanks, in advance, God.

Trail Log: Day 1

The Suffering of Separation

My journey out of the canyon begins today. I've been held up for what seems like years. Rained in. Too hot to walk. Too cold to travel. Alone, I guess. That's it. All alone. I feel separated from everyone and everything these days. From other people. From places that I've loved before. From what makes me happy and joyful. From what makes me sad. From what makes me even feel. From me, too, actually. I feel separated even from you, God. Even you. Who knew? Even you.

Your Bible tells me that your people felt the same way too. Even them. Them, too.

Adam and Eve sought to see themselves as *they and others* saw them. Didn't work out.

Cain and Abel got into it over their need for your acceptance. Only one of them made it.

Noah got out of the flood. Saved his family and the animals. Then felt shame at his nakedness. Maybe he thought that you were ashamed of him, too. You weren't. He was.

Folks tried to create a Tower to raise them up to your level. Not to talk with you. But to see what you see. Hubris run amuck. A whole lot of Babel resulted.

You sent angels to Sodom and Gomorrah. Lot offered his two daughters to the crowd. "Better them than me," he said. I guess he forgot about you, God. Really bad result.

Abraham and Sarah thought that you had cut them off, too. All they wanted was a child. Impatient, actually. Took matters into their own hands. Things got messy from there.

Jacob and Esau started messing with each other. Left you out of it. Cut you off.

Then Jacob and Laban started outwitting the other. Rather than talking with you.

Jacob's daughter got raped. And her brothers sought revenge. They 'gave' it to the rapist. Not over to you. Wild, Wild West justice. Everybody lost on that one.

God's people felt separated. When they really weren't. And it only got worse as a result.

Trail Log: Day 2

The Suffering of Forsakenness

I READ THE CANYON trail guide carefully. I actually studied it. And promised myself to follow it. And then the fog rolled in today. And I lost my bearings. And I got lost. On only my second day. To be honest, I feel totally let down. Forsaken. Off the grid.

So did your people sometimes, God. You told Moses to tell Pharaoh off: Let my people go! And your people got more work as a result. Punished. What is *that* all about? Really?

And then they got out of Egypt. Home free. On the way to the Promised Land. Not really. They complained. A lot. Not enough food. Not enough meat. Not enough water. Never mind that you brought them manna. And quail. And water from a rock. Not spectacular enough? Apparently not. Maybe they wanted room service.

When Moses headed up to Mt. Sinai to confab with God, everyone got jumpy. Felt left alone. Forsaken. Moses came back with the Law. The big one. Ten of them to be precise. And he saw a golden bull that the people had made. Aaron got twitchy. Let 'er' rip, people. Right from the pages of the *Biblical Idol* show. Was cancelled after only one season.

Then, God's people got near The Place, and they sent out a reconnaissance mission. Felt like this was a set-up job by God. Giant people on the other side. Only Caleb and Joshua remembered that God had promised to provide. Everyone else freaked out and lost it.

And God's people were freaking over everything. Rebelled, actually. Mutiny. Even Moses got into the act on that score. Felt forsaken and forgotten. Freaked out. Moses banged on the rock for water. Instead of simply commanding it as God had asked. Oops. Water on. Moses off. Moses got twitchy. Moses stayed behind. See Moses stay. See Moses voted off the island. Or left on the island. Left behind. Then he got dead.

God's people felt forsaken. When they really weren't. And it only got worse as a result.

Trail Log: Day 3

The Suffering of Lost Purpose

It's day three on the trail, God. I'm tired already. I'm already forgetting why I started this trek in the first place. What if the 'hell' that I knew before was better than the one I might end up with anyway? What am I really doing this for anyway? To be honest, I'm not sure.

Your people also lost their purpose in the Bible, God. They got all hung up on ripping through their enemies in the Promised Land. They thought you wanted them all wiped out. Maybe you really said you wanted them all brought into your heart. Missed translation. Bad connection. Oh well. We'll do it our way. I *think* that's what God wanted. . . A pretty hefty body count, I'm afraid. Lots of looting and plundering for nothing.

Oh, and then your people hired some Judges to rule them. And they started this little game. We neglect you, Lord. Then we suffer. Then we cry out to you, God, and promise to repent. And then you spare us from what we were doing to ourselves. Then you save us through a new Judge. And repeat cycle. Then repeat again. Blah. Blah. Blah. Like binge watching the *same* TV show. Over and over and over again. We're talking a lot of reruns here. Who does that, anyway?

And, oh yeah, then Jephthah made a hasty vow to God. Said he would sacrifice the first thing he saw coming out of his home if only God would give his enemies into his hand. Bad promise. It was his daughter who came out first. Dude, the correct answer was count on God's plan. Not on your bargaining power. Turned out really bad for your daughter. Way bad. The worst kind of bad.

Then Sampson got into the act. He counted on his own strength, not God's. And he disregarded his mother's vow. And his own. And God. He got crumpled in the process.

And God's people got into it with each other. They lost their way. And they lost you. God's people felt empty. When they really weren't. And it only got worse as a result.

Trail Log: Day 4

The Suffering of Lost Identity

TODAY, I FELT INVISIBLE on the trail. I looked off into the shrubs and grasses that bordered the trail. And I couldn't tell myself from them anymore. I simply blended into the stuff. And I got off the trail in order to become the stuff. And I got stung. And I got bitten. And scratched. And cut. I forgot what the trail guide said. I got messed up in the process.

Your people lost themselves, too, in the Bible, God. The Israelites demanded a King instead of you. They wanted to be like all the other nations. Instead of yours, God.

Saul turned to his own devices instead of following Samuel's counsel. Instead of waiting on God. The whole Philistines thing didn't work out well either. Because.

Saul messed up again when he turned to a medium to talk with Samuel. More bad news.

Even King David let his ego get in the way. Before he died, he took a census of Israel. Over the objection of David's army commander. King David wanted to know his 'real' military strength. Silly guy. The real strength was in God. Not in David's numbers. And his prize for this little gambit: Plague on the people. Should have counted on God.

So, King Solomon joined in next. He married hundreds of foreign women and fell under their influence. And their idols. And the King got this idea that he needed to build lots of things to be strong. Then he conscripted forced labor. And he taxed everyone to death to pay for it. Like building monuments would create and cement their identity. All it really cemented was their demise. Things went bad. The Kingdom divided into two. And things went downhill from there. Not a pretty sight. King Solomon wasn't so wise after all.

The people of God lost their true identity. And they feuded and schemed and fought. Really messy family food fight. Stuff was flying. And both Kingdoms lost in the end.

God's people felt invisible. When they really weren't. And it only got worse as a result.

Trail Log: Day 5

The Suffering of Lost Control

It's day five today. I'm feeling as if I've totally lost control. The trail goes only one way. All I have is this messed up trail guide. Why should I trust it, anyway? And who's to say that the trail will get me out of the canyon in any event? What if it takes me to some dead end? Some rock wall that I can't climb. In the end. And then I'm ended. For good. Bad.

Your people felt like they lost control in the Bible, too, God. Just like me. Just like me.

The Kingdoms of Israel and Judah were conquered, plundered, and exiled. To far away places. Your Temple in Jerusalem was destroyed in the process. Going, going, gone. A pile of rubble where people once sacrificed and worshipped. Bulldozed. Flattened. And there was nothing the people could do about it. Strong-armed by stronger arms. Way stronger arms, actually. Not God's arms, though. Not for the moment, at least.

Later, your people rebuilt the Temple. But here we go again. It was desecrated by outsiders. Again. And they outlawed your people's sacrifices. And said 'No' to the reading of the Law of Moses. There goes your identity. Again. They shut down your voices. Censured! So much for the Bill of Rights. Cut the cable. Blackout the Scripture Channel. Oh, and your people were now supposed to offer pagan sacrifices. Can it get any worse?

But then things settled a bit for a while. Some control resumed. But Rome got into the act. The whole Roman Empire thing. And the country of Israel became a Roman province. Talk about loss of identity. This province thing was not all that glitzy. Because Rome held all the marbles. Or most of them, at least. For the moment, at least. News Flash: Don't mess with the Empire. It strikes back. Hard. Mercilessly. With finality! Man, what an identity killer. God's people wanted all the control. Then they lost it.

God's people felt powerless. When they really weren't. And it only got worse as a result.

Trail Log: Day 6

The Suffering of Fear

All day today, I've been reflecting on my fears. What if I don't ever get out of this place, this canyon? What if I actually die in here? Who would even find me? How long would I lay there? How long would I have to suffer there alone before I actually... you know, died? Even if I were to be carried out, what would be left of me... you know, my soul?

They talk a lot about fear in the Bible, too. Joseph feared the pregnancy of Mary. He even thought about breaking off their engagement. To spare Mary a certain disgrace. Big time.

When Jesus was subsequently born, King Herod got major paranoid over the prophesy thing. He ordered the killing of all male children two years and younger in the vicinity.

Mary and Joseph didn't like the numbers and got out of town fast. In fact, got all the way to Egypt. They didn't wait for the 4:00 p.m. stagecoach. They simply got after it, pronto.

Years later, Herod Antipas got an anxiety attack over John the Baptist. Seems like John was getting under Herod's skin for Antipas' marrying his own brother's wife. Nasty stuff. In order to make the noise stop, Antipas killed John. Even nastier move, Herod Antipas.

Jesus' own hometown of Nazareth refused to accept him as the Messiah. Jesus rebuked them and the locals tried to kill Christ. They got scared. They lost their heads. Brutal.

Later in Jesus' ministry, the Pharisees and Sadducees got nervous, as well. Seems as if they were twitchy about the messages and actions of Jesus. Jesus was swimming against the current. They wanted to send him down the current. Whitewater. Class 4 rapids.

Later, the Romans got into it too. They got nervous about keeping the peace at Passover. This Jesus guy was stirring things up. Maybe even a revolt. Even Peter denied Christ. Three times, mind you. And we all know how it ended for Jesus. On the Cross.

God's people felt fearful. When they didn't need to be. And it only got worse as a result.

Trail Log: Day 7

The Suffering of Persecution

SO, WHY ARE YOU persecuting me, God? What did I ever do to deserve being stuck in this canyon? It's cold and wet much of the time. I spend too much time waiting it out in the shelters. There's rarely enough wood to make a good fire. I'm worried about running out of food. I feel really, really put-upon here, God. Hello. Is anybody listening to me?

I remember reading in the Bible about how things went down after Christ died. The disciples Peter and John were arrested when Peter cured a crippled man in the name of Jesus. Locked up.

It got even nastier for Stephen, one of the seven appointed to support the disciples. He got stoned. And I don't mean high on pot. Literally stoned to death.

And the fledgling church was persecuted big time. Many saw the writing on the wall and fled quickly. Run for your very lives. Or you'll end up like Stephen.

Peter and James were later arrested and imprisoned by Herod Agrippa I. James was executed. Getting bad fast.

Then, the Apostle Paul came along. He persecuted the followers of Christ, but later heard from the Spirit of Jesus—"Why are you persecuting me?" Paul got the message.

Paul got some of his own medicine during his evangelizing ministry. He was forced to flee more than once. He faced his own persecution and trials in his missionary journeys. Paul even stirred up a riot of craftsmen in Ephesus around the making of idols. He got voted off the show. Completely booted off. No lovely parting gifts, either. Gone.

Paul got into it again when he returned to Jerusalem. Seems as if there was a plot against him. Get Paul in an ambush. Surprise attack. Paul just couldn't seem to stay out of harm's way. They sent him to Rome, where he was arrested again. And he died. Persecuted.

God's people felt hated. When they really weren't. It was the idea of Christ that people were persecuting, really. And it only got worse as a result of taking it personally.

Trail Log: Day 8

The Problem with the Biblical Voices

So, here I am, one week into my journey out of the canyon. I came across some berries today in a beautiful field adjacent to the trail. Just like the trail guide said. It was good to finally eat something fresh for a change. And sweet. I found myself looking at the trail guide, and I reread the thing about not traveling alone. Always staying together in groups. Well, now, that's impossible. I'm a group of one. And then I wondered about God's people suffering in the Bible. And the notion that they really weren't cut off from God. They just *thought* they were. And it only got worse. What if God's people were looking in the wrong place? Like having the wrong trail guide for the canyon trail you're on.

God's people sought, journeyed, traveled, fought, conquered, and settled-in based on their own limited sense of God. Maybe, just maybe, they sought things *from* God instead of simply wanting and waiting *for* God. In the process, they got ahead of God.

And they forgot that God is all-in-all. They were looking for places and people and things. In the process, they forgot that their very essence and being were in God. And God in them.

And then I thought about Jesus. He did a lot of things. Good things. Powerful things. But Christ could only act because he *was* first and foremost. He was, therefore he acted. Not the other way around. Not he acted, therefore he was. Big difference. Major league.

Jesus looked to God for his identity and purpose. Not to some fancy printed trail guide. The trail guide was already *in* Christ. Embedded GPS. Forever batteries. Always charged.

And Christ told us straight. God's Reign begins *in* us. Long before it can be built *through* us. The divine spark of light in us is what lights the way, not the external voices that we usually rely on. So...what if I set my compass each day by God's North Star in me? Then I wouldn't feel so separated, forsaken, lost, purposeless, scared, and persecuted.

Trail Log: Day 9

Listening to God's Voice

TODAY WAS A GOOD day. The best one so far. I found more berries and even some nuts to eat. I feel full. I came across a pretty and calming stream. And I simply sat by it for the longest time. I lost track of time, and taking a break was just what I needed to do today.

And I thought about what God told us in the Bible. God spoke to Moses in the Book of Exodus at the burning bush. Moses was getting nervous about getting 'in the grill' of Pharaoh. The 'let my people go' thing. And Moses asked God an important question.

"So, God, I'm going to your people to tell them your plan for them. Just like you asked me to. Now, they're going to ask a lot of questions about this one. Who am I supposed to tell them sent me?" God didn't give a long, winding, or pontifical response. God simply answered, "I Am Who I Am." God didn't give God's waist size, hair color, preferred toothpaste brand, or shoe type. God didn't list God's prior accomplishments, either. God simply said "I Am." God's power and might were in God's very being and essence.

Later in the Bible, Jesus said, "I do nothing on my own, but speak just what the Father has taught me." Now, Jesus was active for sure. No denying that. But Christ's identity was in the essence of his being in God, through God, and for God. Not himself.

And if that wasn't enough, the last book of the Bible sums it all up quite nicely. Revelation states that God said, "I am the Alpha and the Omega. Who is, and who was, and who is to come, the Almighty." Wow. More of that 'being' stuff. Not a litany of actions. Not a list of credits at the end of a movie. Not a long speech thanking all God's people. No. Rather, simply that everything makes sense only in our very being in God.

Our pasts, our presents, and our futures rest in being in God. Then, no matter what happens, we're not alone. We're not without. We're held gently. . . with and by God.

Final Thoughts for This Leg

THANK YOU, GOD, FOR helping me to finish the first leg of this canyon trail. I thank you for the many voices of the Bible. These voices of your Word tell me that I'm not alone. Not alone in my suffering. For to suffer is to have lived. Lived as human beings. Your people have faced the pains of separation, forsakenness, lost purpose, lost identity, lost control, fear, and persecution. Along this leg, I've learned that listening to these voices *does* matter. I need to listen closely to them. To what they were feeling. And why. For they felt vulnerable, even knowing that you were there. And they opened up to you in every way. They expressed themselves and their feelings to you. Their trials to you. Their doubts to you. Their fears to you. Their hopes to you.

But Lord, I need to read your Word not just from your perspective, but from the mouths of your people, as well. In history. In time. In their places and in their times. I need to place myself more in *their* shoes. Their sandals. Their dusty, dirty, and tired feet. I must be more mindful. Curious and transparent about what their stories of suffering stir up in me. For, in some ways, their journey is my journey. My journey is their journey. While not the same, we jointly share the journey of human suffering. That journey makes us brothers and sisters in the canyon. Let us, therefore, learn from each other. Let us join with each other. Let us look to you with each other. Look to you for guidance, grace, sustenance, strength, and comfort. Look to you to speak not only in your sacred Word in the Bible. But to continue speaking with us even now. In many ways. In all ways. For all times. Through all things. Forever. I'll keep watching and listening, God. Amen.

Canyon Trail Leg Two:
The Problem with our Suffering Voices

"Lord, let me know my end, and what is the measure of my days; let me know how fleeting my life is. You have made my days a few handbreadths, and my lifetime is nothing in your sight. Surely everyone stands as a mere breath. Surely everyone goes about like a shadow. Surely for nothing they are in turmoil; they heap up, and do not know who will gather."

PSALM 39: 4–6

Leg Two Canyon Trail Preview

LORD, I'M ABOUT TO embark on the next leg of my trek in this canyon. The trail map tells me that this leg is more treacherous than the last. While it told me to stay strictly on the path for the past leg, it *now* tells me that it's easy to lose my way on the trail itself. The path is not well marked on this leg. And the path, itself, winds incessantly. With lots of switchbacks. And sheer cliff drops. Not at all easy. And, to add insult to injury, the visibility is often poor— as the trail is generally shrouded in fog and mist. So, it all sets up nicely, don't you think, God? Good chance of getting lost. Taking a wrong turn. Better chance of falling off a cliff. Big fall. Long fall. At least I'll never see it coming in the fog.

I hear my own voice screaming within me on this leg. Everything inside of me tells me not to take this leg at all. Lots of voices. Loud ones. Screaming ones. Screeching ones. None of them real positive, to be honest. I'm, therefore, thinking that I need you more than ever here, Lord. I need to hear *your* voice on this leg of the trail. I need to hear your voice of clarity. Your voice of careful navigation. Your voice of safe passage. Your voice of vision and direction amidst the confusion of it all. In the fog and in the mist and on the narrow turns of this place. I ask you to steady my feet under me and to keep me on track. Please, Lord. Steady me. Thanks, in advance, God.

Trail Log: Day 10

Lack of Feeling Vocabulary

So I've now entered the next leg of this trek out of the canyon. From the looks of the trail guide, it's only going to get worse from here. This is a complete mess. Why did I even start this in the first place? Bad. Bad is what it is. I'm screwed. Toasted. Why bother?

And I'm talking to myself about it all. Talking to myself on a piece of damp paper in this daily journal. If I were to listen to me, I would hear words without feelings. 'Bad'. 'Screwed'. Not feelings, actually. I wonder if that's what makes my suffering so bad? I suffer without real words. My suffering vocabulary is really bad. There's that 'bad' word again. Unhelpful. This stinks, this bites, this is totally unfair, this is the end, and this is undeserved. Not feeling words. Not even close.

How am I really feeling right now? Huh...Well, I'm feeling angry. Angry at the unfairness of my situation. Angry that it happened... I'm feeling sad. That I'm all alone in this bloody canyon. Stuck here trying to get out... I'm feeling forsaken and rejected. That no one understands what I'm going through now... I'm feeling scared. Scared to death, actually. That I might actually die out here... I'm feeling lonely. If only someone were walking with me. Some company for me... I'm feeling broken. Broken by the weight of my pain, suffering, and loss. Busted up... I'm feeling hopeless. Left despondent by the sheer enormity of things crushing on me.

Frankly, I'm grasping desperately for the words that might help me. Any words. Words that might help others to help me, as well. Better words than usual. Much better. The 'feeling' words. The words that sit directly underneath the unsaid bad stuff.

Feeling words won't carry me out of the canyon. I get that. But it's a start. A real start. For when I can 'name' and describe my feelings better, I can better deal with them. I need to better engage with those feelings before I can start to engage with me.

Trail Log: Day 11

Lack of Active Listening

HERE'S THE THING I notice most along this trail. The utter lack of sound. 'Crickets'. Nothingness. Silence. I'd give nearly everything to hear the sound of a bird. Even one. Or the call of a coyote. Even one. Or the chirp of a ground squirrel. Even one. Please.

Actually, I don't even hear the crickets. What I hear is total silence. Until. . . I actually start listening. To the wind. To the silence. Silence has a sound. If I'll simply listen.

The problem with my suffering is like this: I'm listening only to the words that I speak. Or those words that others speak to me. The actual content of the words. Using my brain.

What if I listened to myself and to others with different ears? More actively listen.

What if I listened to the feelings underneath the words—you know, the mad, sad, glad, afraid, forsakenness, and hurt that sit *within* the words? And thought deeply about what those feelings actually mean. This would be active listening at a new and deeper, second level. I suppose it would be harder to do. Harder to stay present at the level underneath. But it might help me to better understand me. And others. And that's that. Actually, no.

What if I listened *even more* deeply? To not just the feelings, but also to the affect. Mine. And others. Like my body language. My facial expressions. My breathing. My tone of voice. And the same for the person I'm talking with. Wow. Now that's even harder. Not sure I can concentrate that much. But what if doing so helped me to really understand what I'm going through? Or he or she is going through. What if the real suffering isn't in the content? But in the feelings and the affect.

What if the real language of suffering is not in the symptoms, but in my response to it? The symptoms are the tip of the iceberg. The thing that wrecks the ship is below the surface. As a result, I need to spend more time there. For, in the deeper waters, lies the truth of my suffering. My loss. And my pain.

Trail Log: Day 12

Lack of Real Communication

MY SUFFERING IS A lot like walking this lonely trail. Even if I try to listen more actively, there's nobody actually talking *with* me. Oh sure, I get talked at all the time. By this trail guide. By the signs along the way. By the occasional guardrails along the sheer cliffs. So I don't fall in. When I do hear from someone, it's always one-way. Like a cell phone without a talk button for me. Like every call I receive starts with this: "Listen up. Just listen. Not a word out of you. Yeah, you." Their way. One way. Or the highway.

And then it gets worse. When I actually get a word in, it's like everyone's got earplugs on. They nod and smile. They look like they're listening. But they really aren't. It's like they've already made up their minds about me. Without me. Without my input.

And when people don't listen to and with me, they don't respect me. It's like I've been discounted. 50% off sale. Every day. Everything must go. Mostly me. I must go. Now. Like I'm a bother because I'm suffering. Check the box and check me out. Over and out.

So far, you're not listening to me. Therefore, you're misunderstanding me. Therefore, you're not respecting me. And therefore, you don't care about me. If you don't listen to my content, my feelings, and my affect, you cannot be empathetic. I might as well be yelling into an empty canyon. When I do, all I hear is an echo. The echo of my own lonely voice. "Hello ... hello, hello, hello." "Hello... hello, hello, hello." Repetitious.

Hearing only my own voice gets old fast. The content of those words goes unheard. When it happens to me, I feel lonely. Alone. Despondent. Angry. Afraid. These are Feeling words. And my Affect becomes withdrawn. I check out. Why bother at all, really?

If only others would truly listen at levels below my content, I might hang in. Hang on. I might feel hopeful. I might feel even courageous. Even confident. Even peaceful.

Trail Log: Day 13

Lack of Trust

WALKING THIS TRAIL TAKES a lot of trust. I need to trust the trail map. I need to trust my compass. I need to trust the counsel that I received before I started this trek. I get a lot of input from all kinds of sources. And that's the way it feels when I suffer, am in pain, or experience a significant loss in my life.

This trail is like a trial. I feel like I've been handed off to some complicated network of 'experts'. They all have their opinions. Everyone has an answer, so it seems. And everyone tells me that they understand. How could they? They're not me. They cannot be me. They actually have *no* idea about what I'm going through. Even though they tell me that they do.

Everyone's an expert about my suffering. Everyone has advice for me. It's like looking at my trail guide in six hundred languages. Like taking the advice of people who've never actually walked with me. Not even a step.

And if that's not bad enough, I feel like I'm always passed around. Like a football in a last minute charge to the end zone with no time left on the clock. Player A hands off to player B. Who laterals me to player C. Who flips me into the air to player D. Who passes me backwards to player E. Who fumbles me on the 30 yard line. Game over. My suffering is like that. Like walking this canyon with a thousand gadgets that don't talk to each other.

But what if everyone 'in charge' of caring for me actually got together and talked? To each other. And came up with a sensible and unified message for me? Instead of this endless babble of input that I can't understand. Came up with some real direction for me. What they will do for me. What I must do for me. How others can help me. That would simplify things for me. And give me a greater sense of trust. In others. That would reduce my stress. And reduce my confusion. And reduce my being reduced. I might even be a 'person' again. Not a football handed off in a futile goal line charge.

Trail Log: Day 14

Lack of Urgency

I FINALLY RECEIVED A cell signal today. Seemed like forever to actually get one. I talked to the Ranger. I told him that I was feeling scared, lonely, tired, angry, and potentially desperate. To get out of this place.

After the Ranger handed me off to a number of 'experts', I was placed on hold for 20 minutes. The wait music was OK. But I didn't appreciate all the happy song lyrics. I'm not happy. Why should anyone else be? And then I got some recorded message stating that I'm important. They're sorry for the longer-than-expected wait time. Asking if I wanted them to call me back. No. Don't cut me off, I thought. Please do not cut me off this call. They didn't. And so I waited some more. . . way more.

Where's the urgency here? I'm suffering. Everyone tells me that they understand. Then they act like this is just not that important. News Flash: It is. Why is everyone moving in slow motion? Why am I kept waiting as if I'm not important? Inconsequential, actually.

Walking in this canyon is like dealing with an insurmountable loss, a crushing pain, a steady dull ache, and an emptiness in my very soul. Everything has changed in my life. Everything similar and comfortable and status quo just went un-quo. 'Un' squared.

And I'm treated like I'm in a waiting line for a hotdog and soda during the seventh inning stretch at the ball game. Just give me the soda, for Pete's sake. Forget the hot dog.

And when I finally get through to an expert, it's a recorded phone tree. "Dial 1 if you're lost in your suffering. Dial 2 if you're really lost. Dial 3 if your pain level is a 10 on the 1–10 scale. Dial 4 if this can wait until the next business day." No option to speak to a human being. Staff cuts, you know. Everything's tight these days. Automation rules.

When I'm kept waiting and waiting and waiting, I feel like nobody cares. Even by the recorded phone message that apologizes for my long wait. And says I'm important. Not.

Trail Log: Day 15

Lack of Individuality

I LOOK AROUND THIS canyon as I walk. I seem to blend into the horizon. The sky is so wide and high. The grey and sandy canyon walls seamlessly mesh with the dirt and brush that bear them up. It's not hard to imagine my being taken into my surroundings. Right now.

Where am *I* in all of this? Have I lost myself? To my surroundings. To the cloudy skies.

My suffering feels a lot like this. When I'm in pain and seek the help of others, I literally give myself to them. Everyone's an expert these days. I don't understand a thing they tell me. Every word feels foreign to me. 'Terms' have replaced language. Technocrats rule.

I have trouble making eye contact any more. It's not that I don't want to. I really do. But no one looks at me. They look away. At screens. At tablets. At charts. At paper.

It's like they're having a séance with their monitors. Hypnotized by data. Input. Output. Key it in. Spit it out. Date of birth. Full name, please. Nature of last surgery. Medications taken. Personal histories. Chronic conditions. Next of kin. Emergency contacts. Mobile phone. Work phone. Home phone. Who has a home phone anymore, anyway?

"Hey. I'm here. In the flesh, buddy. In person." Who could be more important than me? I thought this was about me. I guess not. It's about the bureaucracy, stupid. The machine. The tests. The results. The prognosis. The possible complications. The risks. The benefits. The goals of care.

"Oh, and by the way, your name and date of birth please. Let me scan your hospital bracelet one more time. The computer must be acting up today. New system just installed. You know. The typical glitches. Not to worry, though. There are only 231 people with your same name in our systems."

Suffering is bad enough as it is. And then you get caught in the system. The bureaucracy. And then you get lost. Like you lost your wallet or ID. Disappeared. Your individuality. Your personhood.

Trail Log: Day 16

Lack of Coping

It's been a brutal slog today. Hot. Humid. Desolate. No end in sight. None whatsoever.

This canyon walk is now getting to me. This loneliness is really getting to me. Every part of my body aches today. Even my toenails hurt. Even my hair hurts. My eyes sting. My throat is dry and parched. My nose is clogged up with dust. I need a drink. Not water. Not an energy drink. A real drink. High test. Please. Something to make the pain and sorrow go away. Wash away. Wash over me. If only for a night. If only for a day. I'm angry, frustrated, sad, scared, and lonely.

I need a friend. I'm desperate. A bottle could be a friend. Even my best friend at the moment. Or a pain pill. Or pills. I could smoke some tumbleweed. I'm not even picky anymore. Anything will do. As long as I don't have to feel these things any longer. Even if for only an hour. Or the day. Or a week. Or the rest of this blasted trip out of the canyon. Those things would numb me. Soothe me. Comfort me. Calm me. Put me out.

I'm wondering, though, if that's a false choice. A drink would help me cope, I think. But would it really help? Cope with what? Masking things doesn't make them go away. The things don't go away. They merely hide behind the bottle. They only mask the stuff.

And then the stuff returns. Like my unwanted school chum who keeps calling me. Asking me for money. Another 'loan'. To borrow my power saw. A few dollars for some coffee. Opening my wallet makes him go away. For the moment. But then he's back tomorrow. Mooching on me for more.

Maladaptive coping behaviors are a lot like my old buddy from school. Giving into him only makes it worse. Take a hike, bro. Hit the road. The drink I want most right now doesn't solve anything. The bottle only makes it worse. Because it distracts me from facing the real problem. The one underneath the bottle's label.

Trail Log: Day 17

Lack of Any Feeling

I WOKE UP ON the hard ground this morning. I think I walked too far and long yesterday. Yesterday, I hurt all over. Today, I feel nothing. I have no feeling in my legs and feet. It's scary, actually. At least when it hurts, I feel something. I complain about it hurting. Now I'm terrified that nothing hurts. I'm now numb. Totally numb. Nada feeling. When I feel nada, I can't walk. I can't move. I simply lay there. In the dirt.

My suffering is a lot like that. The people who care for me see my suffering as some wires having gone haywire. Like everything was going fine. . . until the circuits in my body got misaligned. Shorted out. Must have started a fire in my belly or something.

So they called the fire department. And they came to my body and started shooting a fire hose inside me. It wasn't water. Or some chemical to put out the fire. It was some chemical, to be sure. But it doesn't put out the fire. It doesn't extinguish anything, really. It merely 'manages' my symptoms. They call it medicine. I call it over-prescribing.

There's a pill or an injection or some liquid for everything. And I'm left with a list of drugs two pages long. I have to organize them in some pillbox that has numbers and days of the week on it. My biggest worry has become messing up Tuesday with Saturday.

Taking this med instead of that one. Now I have a headache from worrying about all the pills. Maybe I need a new prescription for my headaches. And a third page for my meds list. And a new, larger pillbox to store them in. And a Meds Assistant to help me manage this mess.

Thank goodness for my drug store loyalty card. I get a coupon for $2.00 off soap and toothpaste after filling fifty prescriptions. And $5.00 in instant rewards cash after one hundred. I should be happy. But I'm not, to be honest. Not even a little bit.

I'm simply too numb to feel anything these days. And I need to fill another script.

Trail Log: Day 18

Lack of Curiosity

So, I finally got on my feet after lying in the dirt all day yesterday. I think I may finally have some feeling back in my legs and feet. So, it's onward again. That's that. I thought about the reason for my numbness. But it got too complicated. I think I let the numbness go to my head. I decided to get on with it.

My own suffering is much like that. I quit being curious about it a long time ago. I quit asking the real questions about why I was feeling like I was. Questions like what my thinking, doing, and coping say about what's underneath it all? What's wrapped inside my suffering and loss? I quit going beneath the surface of things...

I stopped exploring the built-in assumptions that I'm making about my suffering. The assumption that this is all my own fault. Or it's never going to get better. Or that I can't cope without help from stuff that never works anyway...

Further, I quit examining my underlying fears along the way. What am I really afraid of here? Maybe I'm scared that I'll look weak. Or that I'll be rejected because of it. Everyone might abandon me. Discard me. Forget about me. Because I'm sick...

Next, I stopped thinking about what my feelings say about my unspoken needs in the midst of my suffering. It occurred to me that I sometimes do certain things because I need certain things. Like I meet everyone else's needs along the line because I need them to like me. If I tell them I'm sick and can't help them, they'll quit liking me. And I need to feel wanted and loved and included. But that's not really true...

Lastly, I stopped thinking about the secrets that I'm hiding from others. The untold stories that I hold most tightly to me. That I guard so incredibly close to my heart and never let out. That I keep under wraps like cash under a mattress. Or ten bars of gold in an armored truck. But it wasn't really gold. In all of this, I dumbed it down. And I dumbed *me* down in the process. Way down. Way bad. Too bad.

Trail Log: Day 19

Lack of God

I WOKE UP STARTLED in the middle of the night. I had dozed off, shifting from one side to the other on the hard soil and rock beneath my back. Then a coyote howled. And howled.

Then others joined in. A virtual cacophony of noise. Like a dissonant orchestra of many instruments. None in the same tune. Different songs. Different pitches. Disconcerting.

And then the birds chirped in. It sounded like everyone was getting into the act.

And then my own voice added to the chorus. I was yelling at all the voices to stop. "Shut up," I yelled into the night. "Just shut up, please." Then I screamed, "Knock it off!"

And then I mouthed some juicy explicative language that I can't repeat in this company. But nothing changed. My own dissonant voice merely added to the jumble of the others. Making it all louder. And even more disconcerting. And I was, by now, wide awake and scared.

But then I looked to the sky. The bright night sky. And I noticed the stars there. They made no noise. They didn't scream, or howl, or whine, or cry out. They simply were there. And when I tried to 'hear' what the stars were saying, I 'heard' energy. Calmness. Peace. Majesty. Light. Comfort. Something bigger than me. Something now, and yet everlasting.

And I thought about God. Who created the stars and the sky and the night. And the canyon. And the creatures. And others. And me. All of them. All of me.

And I wondered, for the first time, whether the problem with all the voices of my suffering is this: That they crowd out the one voice that can actually help me? Help me out of the canyon of my suffering. I've ignored the best voice because that voice didn't scream at me. It was like the voice of the stars. Quiet but powerful.

I thought about God for a change that night. The howls and screams and chirps ceased. All grew silent and I closed my eyes. God was there with me. And I slept. Deeply. Peacefully. Soundly.

Final Thoughts for This Leg

LORD, THANK YOU FOR your abundant mercies and grace, your insights, your guidance, and your direction these past days on this leg of the trail. It's not been easy, to say the least. I've thought a lot about the voices of suffering. Those of others. And of my own.

So many times, the voices of those here to help me don't really help me at all. It's hard to hear my own voice over the din of so many others. I don't feel heard. I don't understand. I don't know where to go with it all. I don't feel respected. I don't feel in control. I don't feel taken seriously. I don't see the urgency in how people respond to me. I've lost the plot. And, as a result, I find it hard to trust. Hard to trust either myself or others, to be honest. I'm caught in this massive messy cyclone of pain.

I need to keep one 'voice' of suffering closer in all of this. That would be yours, God. For too long, I've tried to dull the pain, run from the pain, hide the pain, deny the pain, obscure the pain, transfer the pain, manage the pain, and sometimes give into the pain. In the process, I've closed myself to others and to you, Lord.

Help me to listen more intently and selectively on this journey of suffering. Help me to tune out the racket with more regularity. Help me to tune into One voice far more often. Unlike the other voices, yours is often softer. It doesn't scream or yell. The volume is lower. It's hard to hear you over the noise that surrounds me. But I need to try to turn *your* sound up, God. I need to put on some headsets and move to *your* sound. Your rhythm. Your beat. Your voice. Your music. The music of life. Yes, the music and beauty of life even in the midst of my suffering. Amen.

Canyon Trail Leg Three:
The Roots of the Problem

"O Lord, you have searched me and known me. You know when I sit down and when I rise up; you discern my thoughts from far away. You search out my path and my laying down, and are acquainted with all my ways. Even before a word is on my tongue, O Lord, you know it completely. You hem me in, behind, and before, and lay your hand upon me. Such knowledge is too wonderful for me; it is so high that I cannot attain it."

PSALM 139: 1–6

Leg Three Canyon Trail Preview

ARE YOU THERE, GOD? Can you hear me? I'm ready to start Leg Three of this canyon trail. I can't get out of here fast enough, frankly. And, according to my trusty canyon trail map, this next leg of the trail is going to be a real doozy. It says on the map that the leg is full of dangerous outcroppings. The roots of the trees along the trail have surfaced throughout. These roots jut out of the sand and dirt. It's hard to see them. Because they blend in so well. And they create a real hazard. A good chance of tripping and falling along the way.

So much for the roots. Now onto the rocks. While it's easier to see the rocks on the trail, they're often loose. They shift under my feet. Yep. Yet another chance to trip and to fall. So the forecast for this leg is mostly cloudy—with periods of sprained ankles, cuts, bruises, and scratches. I'd like to ask you for some shin guards and some knee pads, God. To brace me for the falls. But I don't think that's possible. I guess I have to take my chances. Yippee.

What I can realistically ask you for is this, Lord: Please lend me your shoulder along the way. Help keep me upright. And give me sharper eyesight. To see the hidden roots on this trail as I walk. Help me to notice the outcroppings of rocks *before* I reach them. Help me to feel the changing contours of the trail. Give me a sense of what's underneath my feet. Before I actually walk upon the spot. Help me to see the hidden 'markers' of trouble before I can actually see them. Then keep me balanced. Please, Lord. Thanks, in advance, God.

Trail Log: Day 20

My Transference to God

I'VE BEEN THINKING ABOUT God while walking the trail the last few days. And I've come to the realization that I need more 'God' in my life. In my suffering and pain. In my journey out of the canyon. I guess I've always had God. But I've had this sense that the God I had was not *my* God. It was the one I've been told to worship. And the God who's responsible for everything that happens—good, bad, and otherwise. Even the stuff that I do or don't do.

And then I thought, what if I flipped the script here? What if I looked at my *own* experiences of life, suffering, death, dying, and salvation as the starting points for my thinking about God? Instead of what everyone else keeps telling me to think, believe, and do. After I beat myself up for a few minutes about this potentially blasphemous thought, I gave myself a break. I didn't get struck down by some stray lightning bolt. A boulder from Heaven didn't come rolling down on me. The sky didn't turn black. I wasn't besieged by locus.

No. I felt peace. And, in the process, I freed God from all the stuff that I've been taught that I *have* to believe— in order to really 'believe', if you know what I mean. Wow. God just got sprung from the box that we place God in. A God whom I needn't define or limit. For the first time in a long time, I could approach a God who transcends everything we humans attribute to God. Mind-boggling. What's more, I could come to God simply as 'me'. My little ole self. The one who's inherently worthy and special. The one whom God has always been in. From the get-go.

To be honest, it was easier keeping God in a box. And to look to God as being responsible for me. But I know now that it's a cop-out. It's a way of hiding behind my religion. A way out of being me and accountable as me. It's been at the root of the problem all along.

Trail Log: Day 21

God Versus Chaos

YESTERDAY WAS A BAD day. I woke up exhausted. Not a good start. When I began to walk, loose rock moved under my feet. Despite my efforts to stay upright, I quickly lost my balance and came crashing down on a number of large, jagged rocks. One of the rock edges ripped through my pants at the knee and badly bruised my leg. The pain began as mild, but it increased as the day wore on. Why does this stuff happen to me? Why did God place those rocks so loosely in such a difficult part of this trail? It's hard to count on anything anymore. It all feels chaotic, to be honest.

But then I thought: What if the problem isn't the chaos, but how I look at it? What if God didn't move those rocks after all? Maybe they were loosened by years of flowing water, runoff from winter snows, or even the wind. Maybe the ground simply shifted over time. Maybe the earth moved.

I feel like the ground has shifted under my life, as well. And the pain of my suffering is literally running out and off of my body. The 'ground' underneath my feet feels pretty shaky. And the hardest part of my chaos is the one that I'd rather not mention. The 'D' word.

Death. What if I don't make it out of this canyon? What if I don't make it? What if I 'D'? My greatest chaos is the reality that I take each breath with no guarantees. The next one may be my last. And that scares me to 'D'. The big 'D'. And I blame God for not pulling me out of this chaos. If only God would do this. . . why did God do that to me? Why God? Why me?

So, then I thought some more as I patched my bleeding knee. Hey, what if God doesn't even want to control everything? God's not checked out. No. But God's not a control freak, either. God is mysterious. God is dynamic. So why shouldn't God's world be the same? What if God isn't acting in opposition to chaos? Rather, God is working within chaos. Helping us right there. Transforming us right there. Before and after 'D'.

Trail Log: Day 22

Life Versus Death

Part One

My hurt knee was awfully stiff this morning. I could feel the throbs as I awoke on the cold ground. When I got up and continued walking, it began to feel numb. Like it wasn't even there anymore. My leg. One minute, the pain wakes me up. A few hours later, the numbness makes it hard to feel anything. Makes it hard to walk when my leg can't feel the ground.

The numbness in my suffering leg reminds me of the numbness that I feel overall some days in this canyon of suffering. Some days feel like death, to be fair. I've caught myself saying, "I don't even care sometimes whether I die here or not." Then I stop myself, feeling crazy guilty for even thinking such a thing. Stop it! It's either life or death, I remind myself. "I simply must live," I say emphatically to myself. Even the thought of death gives me the creeps. And the more I think about that creepiness, the crazier I sound. Because I know that I'm going to die. It's a sure thing. Bank on it.

But then I remind myself about all the other stuff I think I believe. Like I'll live forever. If only I believe. In God. And I'll eventually be resurrected into Heaven where I'll join my friends and family. A good time had by all! Provided that I get past the Pearly Gates. And pass the admission test. Get all those boxes checked. Double-checked. And the Door Person will tell me, "OK, come on in now. Close call for you, but come in." And I ask the guy, "When will my *body* be coming along behind me?" And the guy responds, "That's all too complicated. Just be patient for now."

So I'm now thinking that I'm in limbo in the heavenly interim—you know, between death and resurrection. Disembodied. All because I insisted on never really dying. All because I needed to be immortal as a body. But what if I'm OK dying, then returning in whatever fashion to God? Intact in whatever form. Whole in whatever form. Heck, maybe even formless. Hmmm. . . Interesting.

Trail Log: Day 23

Life Versus Death

Part Two

So now I've got my knickers completely in a twist over this dying stuff. I'm thinking that I Need To Get My New Body In Heaven! My resurrected one. So that I didn't ever really die. So that I didn't ever have to die. So I could be immortal after all. Like God. Immortal. This whole new body suit thing makes talking about death a lot easier.

That's because if you never really die, you don't have to be scared of it. The best plan to deal with death is to deny it. It makes me feel better. It makes everybody feel better. Kind of like saying to another guy, "Sure is nice that we got this little shower today." As we wade up to our knees in two feet of rainwater from the flood. All I need is taller boots to stay dry. The real problem isn't the length of my boots, though. It's how fast the water's rising. But it's lots easier to deal with the boots.

Death is that way. Immortality is easier. Unfortunately, though, not true. So, as I'm hitting my numb leg to wake it up today, I'm thinking that I need to wake up, too. God loves me. Made me unique and special. But that doesn't mean that I need to stay 'me' immortally for all time. If God transcends all matter, all time, and all space as we know it, why do I have to stay 'me' in Heaven? Why isn't returning to God at death enough for me? Why isn't being with God enough? Why isn't becoming 'one' with all things under God's Reign and Plan good enough? Even if I do so without remaining me.

I can be unique and special without imposing myself on God's universe forever after I've gone. I don't need to impose my own anxiety about death, my own notions about eternity on God or on others. I can't really. I'm not in charge of the universe. Not even close. And when I let go of the immortality thing, it frees me up to return to God someday as the same stardust from which I was created.

From one God to one God. Stardust. Not easy to grasp, but worth thinking about.

Trail Log: Day 24

Prayers to God

I'VE GOTTEN SO HUNG up on this dying thing that I can't get it out of my mind. How did all this get started anyway? Yeah, it was the deep cut on my leg thing. The pain thing. My feeling sorry for *me* thing. My need to prop me up when my heart feels down thing.

So, as I was trudging along today, I stopped and bowed my head. And I brought my mind to God and started talking. To God. At least I thought it was to God. I was carrying on for some time. I went down the list of all my troubles. All my problems. My pain. My worries. My sorrows. My regrets. My hopes. My plans. My needs. My hopes. My fears. My pain. I think I said 'pain' more than a few times to God. Wasn't sure if God got that part of my dialogue. I said a few thanks, and then I got right into the meat of things.

I asked for deliverance. For relief from my sore knee. For a good night's sleep. For softer, dryer ground to sleep on. For warmth from the bitter chill of night. For coolness to better hike in. For clear streams to drink from. For berries to eat. And on. And on. I promised God that if God delivered on all those things, I would most definitely turn my life around. If you do this, God, I'll do that. Promise. No fingers crossed behind my back. See? See?

And then it hit me. I was doing all the talking. And asking. And bargaining. For me. God had just become a grand and mysterious bank money machine dispensing cash. Or prizes. "Put your card in the slot. Then wait. Not too long, please. And Bingo!"

On demand. And. . . I was thinking that I had been trying to 'tee God up' by praying only in certain ways, places, or times each day. Routine. Repetition. That's the ticket. And that I had to get the words right for the winning ticket. Until I realized that my talk with God wasn't a dialogue with listening. It had become a monologue. A one-way line. Outward, not inward. Closed circuit. Closed heart. Closed off. From God. That's not prayer.

Trail Log: Day 25

Unholy Alliance

The more I began to realize that my whole prayer thing was messed up, the more I got to thinking about how God might be seeing *me* in the process. I stopped along a streambed this afternoon and looked into the water. Where deeper, quieter pools sat, I saw the reflection of the canyon walls. Of the sky and clouds. In deep, resplendent color. As if God was using these deep and silent pools to mirror whom God really was. Beautiful.

Then my eyes drifted to an area of faster currents. The shallower water seemed to race over the rocks, creating a blurred image, at best. Distorted reflection, actually. I reflected on this non-reflection, and started wondering whom *I* really reflect. And I realized that I didn't look to God much for my reflection after all. I was like the racing, shallow water, pin-balling over the rocks without any apparent direction— influenced wholly by the force of the water and the curvature or formation of the resisting rocks.

The rocks had become my focus on 'others' for who I really am. I wasn't seeking myself in God. Instead, I was trying to outrun the others. Like the rapid stream current trying to outrun the rocks. And I couldn't ever outrun them, I figured out. The rocks were always bigger, prettier, stronger, better, and shapelier than me as the water. And when 'me' as the running water started to question my own inherent strength and reflection, I started to doubt. To mistrust. To feel guilt and shame. To feel inferior. To withdraw. To fuse with the rocks. To isolate myself. To blame myself. To become a victim of the rocks.

And I compensated for all this 'stuff' by putting on a 'mask'. I took on the persona of the rocks, not the beautiful, calm water that I once was. My mask became my reflection in order to conform, please others, be safe, and not disappoint the rocks. And my raging water became rancid. Because I looked outward to others. You know, the rocks. Instead of me.

Trail Log: Day 26

Thing Versus Whole Person

THIS ROCK THING HAS had me very worried over the past day or so. I feel like such a rock-head now. How could I not have seen this before? How in the world could I have spent my life trying to look like a bunch of rocks, instead of the true and brilliant reflection of God already in me in the water?

And because of my distorted vision, I've now come to know that it's made my suffering worse. Way worse, not better. Because when I focused on the rocks, I became a 'thing'. *Person as thing.* People can't be things. But I chose to be a rock. A thing. And in the process, I lost 'me' as a person. I tossed out my birthright as a whole human being.

Now, if that wasn't bad enough (who wants to be a rock?), I started to morph along the way. When I lost me, I started to fuse into my pain. I became my disease. I began to see myself as somehow disfigured and mutilated by my sorrows, suffering, and pain. Literally being disintegrated. Like a rock being cracked open. And when that happened, I started medicating myself to make the pain go away. I became a numb rock, but not a happy one. I quit feeling. Rocks don't feel. Especially when self-medicated.

And when not feeling became my new norm, I started to resist crawling out of my little space. Until I finally realized that I wasn't really my disease, or my pain, or someone else, or a rock. I was the real, whole, and integrated me—mind, body, and soul—a person, not a rock. Hidden and masked sometimes, but there nonetheless. With real potential, gifts and great qualities. Loved.

And I crawled out of my rock hole. And let myself float gently. Wow. I didn't sink like a rock. I didn't because God's reflection in me isn't heavy. I could enter fully and freely into the space of the water without fear, judgment, or comparisons. I could simply accept the freedom and the journey. Without the weight of some rock dragging me down. For, I'm not a thing or a rock. I'm me.

Trail Log: Day 27

Control Versus Freedom

I TOOK THE DAY off today. Decided not to go anywhere. It was hard at first. I've felt the need to cover at least ten miles each day on this walk. Out of the canyon. The sooner I get out, the sooner my suffering will be over. I've had a plan. Precise. Exact. Disciplined. Got this under control. So when I decided to take a break today, I got a little panicked. It felt like I was losing control. That was scary, to be honest.

So, I closed my eyes to calm me down. I breathed deeply. I meditated on control. And I asked myself, what is control anyway? I started to think about all the things that I can really control. I took out some paper and a pen to start a list. This will be easy, I thought. But, the more I thought, the more I realized how little I actually control after all. It dawned on me that my efforts to control things, people, timing, flow, outcomes, results, suffering, grief, and all the other stuff are entirely illusionary. Like thinking that I can find the only ant living in this enormous canyon. Finding that ant takes a lot of energy, and it wastes a lot of time.

But, back to me... When I try to control everything, it closes me off to me and to others. Or it fuses me into them. In order to control. On the other hand, if I give up and give it all to God, I disempower me in the process. So this makes everything about some skewed sense of power. The power to control. Either by me or by God.

But when I came to learn that control is largely an illusion, I actually felt lighter. Freer. Wow. It allowed me to embrace the mystery and randomness of things. It allowed me to join in that mystery with a sense of adventure and awe, not with the need to control it all. And here's what else: I began to understand the power of faith in so doing. Believing that things can somehow work out, even if we don't work it out. And with the power of that faith, the hurts and pain started to flow through me. Not sitting inside me. It made more room for God.

Trail Log: Day 28

Unconscious Versus Conscious

By taking the day off yesterday, I had a chance to purposefully lose control. It felt good, actually. It was the first time I've really 'felt' anything, then 'named' it in a while. So, while I climbed an incline today, I played a game. To take my mind off the climb. I decided to recognize everything I was feeling along the way. Then think about why I was actually feeling them. I felt tired after an hour. So I thought it's because I've walked uphill for an hour. But that wasn't really it. I was tired because I'm exhausted by the sheer weight of my legs straining to defy gravity.

My feelings about my suffering are the same, really. As long as I've been content to numb my pain, to mask it, to deny it, or to fuse it with a ton of other non-related stuff, I've never gotten in touch with what's actually underneath it. But the hidden, weighty stuff underneath it is still there pulling me down. Now, it's acting on me in ways that often make me act out or act on others or to simply act. But it's unconscious. And that makes it far more dangerous for me. It makes me an unconscious incompetent. I don't know what I don't know.

But when I try to bring it to the surface and get curious about it, I resist it. Because surfacing, naming, exploring, and feeling my feelings are painful. And scary. And if I do so, I might fall down. And crash. So I resist. But if I break through the resistance, I exert my will and my courage against the forces that try to bury stuff. I can move the needle on me and become a more conscious incompetent. I stumble, wrestle with things, and feel the pain.

But I get up and become incrementally more consciously competent. Slow, uneven, but sure progress. The journey of raising my unconscious pain to my conscious is not an easy one. It's not a linear one. It's not a tidy one. But it's a necessary one. Because, until I know what I don't know, I don't know anything. That's worth knowing. And feeling.

Trail Log: Day 29

Lost Translation

I STOPPED ALONG THE trail yesterday to rest for a while. This whole notion of unconscious feelings was beginning to overwhelm me. Just like the thought of how far I've yet to go to get out of this place. I was feeling pretty darned frustrated at this prospect when I raised my head and yelled into the canyon. I heard a faint echo of my screaming voice as it bounced off some sheer walls to each side of me. I couldn't make out the words in the echo. As if my voice was lost in translation as it rattled around in mid-air.

My unconscious suffering has been like that, I guess. It's dangerous. When I got to thinking about why that's so, I came to understand this: When I act out my diffused unconscious anger, it nearly always comes out different than it should. And usually to the wrong person at the wrong time in the wrong place. Just plain wrong. It's like an eruption that spills out upside down or sideways instead of straight into the sky. I cope like a maladaptive volcano, spewing lava in some obscure, erroneous fashion. It doesn't help others. It doesn't help me.

For my unconscious coping actions give me no clue as to what the real problem is. It's like a knuckleball thrown at the wrong target. What's worse, it feels like it's working, but it isn't. It actually makes things worse, even if I think they're better. It's like wallpapering over some major cracks. Looks good, kind of. But the cracks keep getting deeper. And because I think it's working, I repeat it. Again and again. As a result, I form my screwball coping into a train wreck of new, long-lasting, rotten, and misdirected cover-up habits ripping up everything around me. And this only compounds my suffering.

In the end, no one is really fooled. Except me. . . until I realize that I've become the fool. Everything gets dinged, except the real problems underneath. And the unconscious cracks beneath the wallpaper keep dangerously spreading. Until I crack. . .

Trail Log: Day 30

Unconscious Origins

I SPENT THE WHOLE day with my head spinning. Trying to bring the unconscious to my conscious was a good deal harder than walking the steep inclines. My feet and legs were tired. My mind and my heart were exhausted. It was like trying to wring water out of a large towel by hand. Hard work. But worth it, I think. Or feel, rather. The stuff that I wrung out of my unconscious was some heavy-duty baggage, I'm afraid.

I never gave much thought to my past to be honest. I've always been focused on coping with today's challenges. My yesterdays have been lost along the way. But I'm coming to realize that the stuff from those yesterdays matters a whole lot more than I might have thought.

I started to reflect on the dysfunction of my family of origin. I remember that no one ever showed much emotion. Life was not a contact sport, feeling-wise. More like solitaire. And I got to pondering whether that's why I've had so much trouble naming my feelings. Or crying in my loss and pain. Because I was never taught to in the first place. Worse yet, because it wasn't acceptable.

And I was taught a bunch of other stuff—truths, if you will. Like I must be strong, no matter what. I must never give up or quit. I need to make something of myself. I should be seen, but not really heard. Like some trophy in a case to gawk at. Further, I need to always make others proud of me. Don't ever, ever disappoint. Hmmm. . . and here's another one: I'm not capable enough. I'm not worthy enough. Great isn't really great after all. It's only good. But great wasn't always unattainable. And good was never good enough. And, therefore, I could never measure up. Because great kept getting in the way of ever being good.

The problem with it all was that I didn't just learn all this stuff. I *internalized it as truth*. The truth. The whole truth and nothing but the truth, so help me God. Help me, God. I need to unlearn some stuff. From way back.

Trail Log: Day 31

Mid-Life

BECAUSE I NEVER SURFACED all the stuff from my earlier life, I never realized that I was living my hurts entirely unconsciously. Huh, I thought I was in control, but I wasn't. The unconscious stuff was. But I was rocking along, coping along, getting on with things. Or so I thought. Until I got sick. Until my best friend suddenly died. Until I lost my job. Until I lost my dog. Or my wife. Or my house. Or my health insurance. Until I landed in this desolate canyon and hit the wall. Boom. No. Boom-Boom!

And when I came to, my head hurt bad. I thought that I had just banged my noggin. "Two aspirin, please." But it was way more than that. I had really banged my soul. I hadn't just lost things. No. Things were flung into a sandstorm and started swirling all around me. My equilibrium got all messed up. I started losing my footing in the blowing dirt. My dreams turned into the sometimes-sour taste of reality. My journey of fulfillment became a stop sign of stagnation. My vitality started to break down. Victories sometimes morphed into setbacks. Advancing years turned my delusion of immortality into the finite reality of my remaining days. Additions and gains lost ground to subtractions and losses. Instead of acting on things, I started to get acted upon. My endless possibilities slid headlong into a growing list of regrets. My bucket list became a dust bucket. Filled with only dust and anger. To be retained, not discarded.

In all of this, my unconscious past and my need for control had robbed me of my ability to re-invent myself along the way. Kept me stuck in my suffering. But hold on here. . . I don't need to see my glass as half-empty. . . or even half-full. No. Instead, I need to create a brand new glass. Something amazing and beautiful and rich. With the pieces of the shattered fragments of my losses. All I need is some glue and my imagination. An ability to be open to the future. To dream anew.

Trail Log: Day 32

Anger Versus Hurt

EARLIER TODAY, I DID something stupid. Really stupid. I got off the trail to hunt for some berries. Along the way, I ended up walking into a snake. The snake rattled. I freaked out. The snake lunged at me. I jumped back. I fell over. Quickly got to my feet and ran. Close call.

After my heart stopped racing, I got really mad. I was proud that I acknowledged my feelings for a change. 'Angry'. That's right. I Was Angry. At the snake. At me. At everything around me today. So, I thought that was good. But was it really? It was easy being mad. It allowed me to control my own dialogue. It allowed me to lash back at that dirty snake. It allowed me to get even.

But the more I kept up my ranting, the more I realized that I'd also stopped listening. While being angry helped me to fume a little, it also kept *me* from taking any ownership. By yelling at the snake for being stupid, I quit asking helpful questions about why this had really happened. In effect, it closed me off to protect me. It created a safety net. A wall. It made the mean snake and the stupid me the problem. Instead of the gaping holes in my berry picking strategy today. Being angry blew off steam, but it didn't inform. It was easy, but wasn't helpful to me. For it was a far too diffused response.

In truth, my anger was probably triggered by something far more significant than a chance encounter with a snake. Maybe it was telling me something deeper. Like I'm feeling particularly lonely and vulnerable today. Like I'm scared that I'm running out of food. Like this reminds me of something that happened to me a few years ago when I was also feeling vulnerable. When someone who I thought was a friend lashed out at me—out of nowhere. When that happened, I felt betrayed, hurt, and overwhelmed. But instead of checking in with my feelings, I simply picked myself up and fled. Got angry. Just like today with the snake. Rattled.

Trail Log: Day 33

Becoming a Victim

LAST NIGHT, I HAD a nightmare about the snake that nearly killed me yesterday. I dreamed that there were ten of them, not just one. They surrounded me. They trapped me in the middle. I couldn't move or run. I could hardly breathe, I was so terrified. I was being victimized by those nasty, killer snakes. They didn't bite me. They simply hissed and showed their slimy fangs. I awoke sweating and paralyzed. And I've felt sorry for myself all day because I'm exhausted by last night's dreams.

It reminds me a lot of my situation in this canyon of suffering that I'm stuck in right now. I'm surrounded by a wall of worry, pain, and sorrow. None of which is really my fault. My loss and pain were handed to me. Not like some prize, but like a hand grenade that was dumped in my lap. I didn't ask for any of it. I didn't want any of it. I wasn't ready for any of it. But 'it' came my way. The violence of this sickness and sadness against my soul became part of me along the way.

It feels like others actually blame me for this mess sometimes. Do you believe it? Like it was *my* fault. I get blamed for not doing enough to stop it. I get blamed for staying in it. As if it was something that I could just leave behind. Like a candy wrapper in a trash can somewhere. I even blame myself.

And when they do and I do, I become imprisoned in my little victim self. Within the walls of my prison, I no longer trust anyone or even me. This means that healthy, loving relationships go down the drain. I think myself as unworthy. I must have deserved it in the first place. In turn, I have to earn the love and trust and respect of others. Or I need to fight back. Real hard. Or even worse, I need to find someone to 'fix' me. Or I need someone to fix. Someone that I can fix. Or I simply quit trying in the midst of my victimhood. And I languish in my prison cell of victimization. Why bother. I'll never crawl out of this mess, anyway. For I'm a victim.

Trail Log: Day 34

Brokenness

As I was trekking the trail today, I saw a pile of shattered pottery under a ledge. The pieces were broken, but had been pushed together as if someone had tried and failed to reconstruct the former thing. The edges of the pieces were jagged and rough. Couldn't have been put together again anyway, I thought.

And then I wondered if this mess of clay might contain a message for me? You know, I'm broken too. Really broken. Especially here in the midst of this vast canyon of suffering. Then my mind raced ahead to brokenness as my 'sinfulness'. I'm broken because I've sinned. Against God. Against my family. My friends and neighbors. Everyone, actually.

And then it slowly dawned on me: What if my brokenness isn't about my sinfulness after all? Rather, it's really about my separation from myself and from others. Caused by my setbacks in life. My disappointments. My losses of family and of friends. The death of loved ones. The job I so wanted, but never got. The friend who abandoned me when I needed her most. . .

However, by treating my brokenness as something I deserved, my inherent sin, I feel angry and guilty all the time. I'm ashamed of myself. And I turn all that stuff outward to others. You know, trying to deflect, marginalize, control, violate, and obscure. You know, share the pain with everyone around me like some toxic hot potato that I need to toss to the guy next to me. When I view my brokenness as my inherent 'badness' as a human being, I shut others out. And even though I ask God to heal me, I really shut God out, as well. Because I need God to fix me.

And, in the process, I ask God only to glue me back together as I 'should' be. Instead of taking the pieces of my true brokenness and making something beautiful with them. Into a new piece of art. Something even more amazing than before. Not knowing this has been at the root of my problem all along.

Trail Log: Day 35

Courage Rather Than Fear

I STOPPED ALONG THE trail and rested before eating something mid-day. There were a bunch of small stones strewn across the spot where I had sat down. After staring at them for some time, I remembered my having thought about brokenness yesterday. So I began to organize the rocks by shapes and sizes. And I slowly created a rock sculpture of sorts. Nothing fancy. But different and interesting. Like a piece of art.

And it occurred to me that I've begun to look differently at things these past few days. Hard work. I've had to come to grips with my feelings. Pushing the unconscious to my conscious mind. It's been tough. But running scared hasn't helped. It's put my focus entirely on real or perceived threats to me. It has left me paralyzed. I've tried to control everything as a result. . . including me. Doing so seemed to give me a sense of security. But it wasn't the real deal. Nope. A façade. An illusion. Like a card trick or some amateur magic act. Smoke and mirrors. Bait and switch. Furthermore, it closed me off as a 'victim'. It got me stuck in the dirt. On the rocks. Hanging on the ledge. By my fingers. Or toes. Or my chinny-chin-chin.

So, what if there's another way, I asked? Perhaps courage *is* that way, I thought. Courage focuses on the opportunity before me. I can move toward something, not run away from something else. Courage also gives me a sense of change. A possibility for something better, no matter how dim the view is right now. Further, courage invites me to engage in the struggle. It invites me to take some risks. It calls me to be transparent with myself and with others. It challenges me to be open and curious, not closed and imprisoned.

In the end, fear is predictable. The best I can hope for is to manage the status quo. Like making the best of a raw deal. Keep it from getting worse. But courage allows something greater. Allows God to work within me. Toward transformation. And hope.

Final Thoughts for This Leg

THANK YOU, GOD, FOR continuing to walk with me. This leg of the trail was particularly challenging for me. I've had to come to grips with some tough realities about myself. And the roots of my suffering problems. It's like I've been living in some parallel universe for way too long. Perhaps we all have. It feels, therefore, like a big one. This parallel place. But it's simply not true.

I've deceived myself about a lot of things through the years. I guess it was easy to do so. Comforting in an unhealthy kind of way, I suppose. I've also hidden behind you in an effort to control everything. I've tried to manage everything until I couldn't—then made myself feel better by turning it all over to you. Like this whole life thing was something that needed to be micromanaged. And while I dumped the mess on you, I never quit praying for all the stuff that I wanted. So. . . I never really let up on the reigns anyway. In the spirit of control, I turned 'me' into a thing. I gave up my freedom. The freedom that you gave me for my 'whole' life.

I've kept so much stuff buried through the years, God. And, when it tried to surface on me, I pushed it right back down. Then I got angry. Instead of being curious about it. Instead of feeling hurt, I simply got mad. Then I lashed out. At others. And at myself. Then I became a victim. Of my own stuff. And I blamed myself for being bad. And, in the process, I got in bed with my fear. Instead of sleeping with my courage. In truth, I made a 'deal with the devil' a long time ago. It's not worked out that well, Lord. I need to unwind this deal.

I need 'voice lessons' from you, God. In order to teach me to talk in a different octave. One that can help me heal, versus continue holding me down. I may have lost my voice. But it's not permanent. Unless I let it be so. Let me speak with your voice, God. I like the sound of that much better. Amen.

Canyon Trail Leg Four:
Our God Problem: Theodicy

"When I look at your heavens, the work of your fingers, the moon and the stars that you have established; what are human beings that you are mindful of them, mortals that you care for them?... O Lord, our Sovereign, how majestic is your name in all the earth!"

PSALM 8: 3–4 AND 9

Leg Four Canyon Trail Preview

Dear God, just when I thought that it couldn't get any more challenging, it's about to now. The trail map has a special alert for this leg of the trail. It characterizes a major portion of the leg as 'remote'. There are few shelters for shade and protection from the winds and the rain. In other words, I'm out in the elements in the middle of nowhere. And to make things more interesting, the map says that this portion of the trail is at a high risk for avalanches. Large, loose rocks above me can shift and tumble. That would be 'onto me'. So, the only thing *not* remote in the days ahead is the chance I'll get rained on, blown away, or crushed by some rocks. From above. That I won't see until they're on top of me. Crashed. On me. Or what was once me. Lord, I can't seem to catch a break here.

Just when I need you most, God, I'm beginning to wonder about you the most. Just checking. Where *are* you in the midst of all of this? I'm about to hear the lashing rain. The gusting winds. The sound of falling rock and stone. But I'm not really hearing *you* right now. I'm asking you to do something here, Lord. Show me something. Get me out of here. Or, at least, get me past this leg of the trail. Without my getting soaked and wind-burned. Without getting smashed by a landslide. Of loose rocks. Lord, please do your thing. Be powerful in this moment. Give me some shelter from the storms that rage around me here. For goodness sakes, please. Thanks, in advance, God.

Trail Log: Day 36

Three-in-One

TODAY HAS BEEN OK so far. It's been warm, sunny, and nice. A slight breeze to keep me cool. Just right. The problem with canyon weather is its unpredictability. One minute it's scorching hot. At night, it's frigid cold. The hot winds burn my face. The cold winds freeze my hands. And I'm powerless to do anything about it. Why must I endure this? Why can't someone help me out here? Why can't God help me out here?

Then I look around the canyon. Its beauty is magnificent. The colors can be marvelous and brilliant. The skies are bigger than life itself. And I think, God did this all. God is truly powerful. God made the canyon. God makes the weather. God blows the wind. God powers the sun. God is mighty. God is stronger than anything. Way strong. Powerful.

Not just powerful, but God is also good. God wants only the best for me. Of course, because God loves me. God loves us all. God loves all things, everywhere. God's goodness means that God loves justice. God wants everything to turn out right. God hates unfairness and suffering. God wants us all to live fulfilled, joyful, and blessed.

But here's the rub. Bad stuff happens. Everyday. Things aren't fair sometimes. Good people get hurt or die or get put upon. Tragedies come along. Violence comes along. Crummy, lousy, hurtful things come along. Evil comes. Then it stays for a long time.

So, if God is all-powerful and if God is also all-good, how can there also be evil and bad stuff? I can't hold all three things together in one. If God is all-powerful and all-loving and good, bad things shouldn't happen. But they do. Evil and suffering are real. All too real. So. . . this means that God is either not all that powerful or not all that good.

I can only hold two of these characteristics about God at once. Never all three. This has me all messed up. Frankly, it stinks. And I'm very, very disappointed. And confused.

Trail Log: Day 37

Hiding Behind God

When I'm having a particularly bad day, like today, I give it all to God. I say happy things like, "God doesn't give me more than I can handle." Or I tell myself, "God knows what's best for me. I just need to trust and obey." Sometimes I convince myself that I have my Cross to bear—just like Jesus did. And I have to carry this Cross with a happy face. It's my burden to carry. And my privilege to carry. Even when I'm too tired to carry.

It's mine to carry because God gave it to me. God's got this whole thing covered. It's all in God's hands and it's all in God's plans. I don't need to worry. Everything I do or say or think or feel is already planned out, mapped out, worked out, thought out. God's got all of it. So, no matter what, I need not question. I need not worry. I need not doubt.

Now, on the one hand, that's somewhat comforting. It makes it easier to lift my arms and legs when it feels like someone's controlling the strings. Like a God-Puppeteer. I simply need to cooperate. Right hand. Left arm. Right knee. Left leg. Lift. Drop. Stay. Dance.

But what's comforting isn't necessarily helpful to me. For trusting God's heart is not the same as giving it all to God to handle. The former is participatory. The latter is abdication. The former is walking in God's love. The latter is hiding behind God's cloak.

The problem may not be in God's power. It might be in how *we* define that power. God's omnipotence doesn't mean that God has to control everything. Or everyone. Or every minute of every day of every week of every year. But, because that's how we define power, we seem to want to relinquish our role in things. In order to have true faith in God. But what if God doesn't want our blind faith? What if God wishes our active faith?

Faith that doesn't give our autonomy away. Faith that doesn't give our life away. Rather, faith that actually empowers us. Powers us. So we can power in and through.

Trail Log: Day 38

Good and Evil

I HAVE TO ADMIT that I'm struggling with the whole bit about God's power. As I was walking along today, I thought things were a whole lot easier when I simply saw God as being in complete control. The Big Boss. The person in control. Who has it all. Command and control. Like the dude in the tower at the airport. "Flight 24/7/365, you're cleared for takeoff on Runway 1."

But, let me put that on hold for a minute. The whole good and evil thing is even more worrisome. God wants only good for us. But evil is a part of us. It's real. And that messes up the whole 3-in-1 God thing. The whole theodicy thing. But what if I'm having the *same* definition problem here, as well? Like I was having with the whole 'power' thing before.

What if the difference between good and evil is mostly in my definition of things? Like some simple equation. Such as good equals right. Bad equals wrong. Straightforward. Neat. Clean. Pure and simple. Yep. All sorted out now! But not all that helpful. Good and evil are, in truth, grey and nuanced. They're not always opposites. When I equate God with good and someone else as bad, I set up false choices. I start thinking in polarized and dualistic ways. I create some zero-sum game in which life is meted out into one pile or another. And, of course, I hang on tightly to my spot on the good pile. Or I impose my good pile views on others. You know, to the people hanging out on the bad pile. Or I try to force them to change themselves. To be more like me... on the good pile.

When that happens, I take power into my own hands in unhelpful ways. And I see God on *my* side. The good side. Or, at least, 'good' as I've defined it... for everyone else. From my spot on the good pile. At least, until I fall off the pile. Fall from my own grace. And I get mad at God and ask "Why God? How can this evil happen to me? I was doing so well." According to whose definition, though?

Trail Log: Day 39

Blaming God

TODAY WAS A TOUGH one. I had to cross a small stream with a rapid current. The water was icy cold. I tripped on some rocks beneath the uneven waters surging around my legs. I went down into the water, but was able to pick myself up. A good thing. And I wrung myself out. Good thing. But I got soaked and cold. I started shivering as the sun went down. Bad thing. Had to build a fire. Good thing. But the wood was wet and didn't burn well. Bad thing. I got mad at God for all of this. I told God I had taken just about as much as I could. I told God I was having real doubts about God's goodness and power.

At first, I felt better. Powerful. I could tell God off. Give God a piece of my mind. Get it off my chest. Let God have it. And God didn't let me have it back. But minutes later, I started feeling crummy. Guilty. How could I get mad at God? Who in the heck do I think I am, anyway? God let me off this time, I figured. But God is keeping a tally of how many times I get mad at God. At some point, I'll hit the magic number. And God will give me Hell. Or send me there. Express service. Non-stop flight.

And besides feeling guilty and afraid now, I started to 'write' God off. You know, if God's not going to help me out more and stand up for what's right, what good is God anyway? I guess I need to do this all on my own. Who needs this God person anyway?

But the more I thought about it, the worse this option became. For, by walking out on God, I was walking out on myself. By rejecting God, I became homeless. Separated. Without God, my life became merely survival. It wasn't really life anymore. In fact, life without God was really death. When I turned on God and left God, I turned on myself. Until I turned back to God. And I realized that, even when I'm mad at God, God would never leave me. God could never hate me. God understood. God could only love me. Let's keep talking, God. Good thing.

Trail Log: Day 40

Ambivalent Feelings Towards God

BECAUSE OF MY FALL into the stream yesterday, I had to spend most of today trying to dry out my clothes—first by last night's fire, then by today's sun. By the time I put some of these clothes back on, I was feeling pretty ambivalent about heading off for the remainder of the day. I knew that I needed to keep moving on, but I had now lost most of my motivation.

So, I sat and looked at the sky for a while. Times of sun fell into shadows, as the sun crept slowly behind grey, forming clouds. It was as if nature, itself, was ambivalent about the kind of day it wanted.

Sometimes I admit feeling the same way about God. It hit me that I never thought much about God growing up. So I had a blank there. But I'm sure that, for others, their early 'feel' for God may have been different. God may have made them feel secure. Safe. Others may have experienced God with anxiety or guilt or even shame. Maybe others looked to God and simply depended on God for everything. Some may have experienced God as empowering, offering confidence. For others, God may have made them angry— wondering what kind of God brings them this kind of misery in their lives.

Maybe we all feel some of these things at various points in our lives, to be honest. And we probably feel them because we learned to feel them from others. From how *they* experienced God. Or how others acted because God was there. . . or in spite of God being there. Maybe, just maybe, God was never spoken of in the house. Or maybe God was. But talking about God always came as a lecture. With a stern voice. Perhaps God was not to be questioned. Or doubted. Or tested. It simply *is* the way God is. It's written. Once and for all. Case closed.

So I may have closed off *my* mind and frozen God, as well. How I think about God right now has a lot to do with what I was taught. Even if I don't recall it. It's still there for better or for worse.

Trail Log: Day 41

The Human Trinity

Part One

Earlier today, I saw what looked like a Cross carved into a rock at the edge of the trail. Could have been anything, I guess. Even a coincidence. Or maybe I've been doing more thinking than usual about God. While I'm stuck here in my pain and loss. As I looked at the Cross, I began to think about the Trinity. You know, Father, Son, and Holy Spirit.

And I got a brilliant idea. Why can't we humans have a trinity, too? A *Human Trinity*. After thinking on this for a while, I had it: The person I wish I wasn't. The person I would rather be. And, finally, the person that I actually am. Three. Trinity. Eureka! The Human Trinity.

Now, the first member is the person I wish I wasn't. It's all the stuff that I'm ashamed of in my life. It's me when I get angry with myself. For all the stuff that I'd rather not do. But I do, anyway. Or it's the 'me' that I am when I feel lonely. Or the 'me' when I start wallowing in my pity party. And the guest list is very, very exclusive. Only I'm invited. "Hi. This is Me." And I respond to myself, "Happy to meet me. Life sucks." And I reply to me in return, "I know what you mean. It sucks. And so do I, by the way." And then I respond to me, "Exactly, brother."

So I and me have this party. And I beat me up. And I drink way too much of the malaise punch. And I get drunk in my worthlessness. Then I get bored with the pity party scene and leave. I try to seek out some better company than myself, but I loathe myself and wish I weren't me. Who would want to hang out with me anyway? No one in his or her right mind. Not even God would want to be with me. It's like I have this yellow police tape surrounding me. The sign says, 'Keep out. Dope resides here.'

And then it hits me. If I wish I wasn't me, then I'm nobody, really. Because me is who I have. If I can't love me, no one else can either. If I can't love me, I can't let God in to love me, either. I must know more than God.

Trail Log: Day 42

The Human Trinity

Part Two

So, THE FIRST PART of my Human Trinity is the person that I wish I wasn't. Got it. But I need two more persons of the Trinity. Trinity implies three, not one. Then I remembered. The second part of the Trinity is the person I'd rather be.

I grew up wanting to be a movie star. A firefighter. An astronaut. The President. Kid stuff, you know. We all do it, I guess. As a kid. But I realized that *I* never grew up. I kept on wishing that I was someone else. Even after reaching adulthood. Now, it's no longer the firefighter or movie star thing. I'm cool with not being them. I can't act worth a lick anyway. I didn't want to be someone else.

But here's the thing. I've never stopped wanting to be *something* else. I've had this idealized picture in my mind of something else. I want to be taller, smarter, funnier, wealthier, happier, cuter, thinner, more successful, more thoughtful, more sharing, less cautious, better on my feet. You get it. But here's the deal. I want to be these things because I'm told that I need to. By others. In truth, I hear this stuff all day long without even knowing it really. Subliminal messaging. It's everywhere around me. So much so that I don't even notice it anymore. But it's buried in my soul. A vague longing or seeking that sits below the surface. Makes me unconsciously aware that I need to be something better. Better than me.

Now in order to be a better me, I, in turn, try to control things more. I hold onto what I seek or buy more tightly. I try to hold back the years. Or the pounds. Actually, I get obsessed with it. Or I try to escape. To go places. Or do things that make me feel like a new man. The one I can't describe but subconsciously can't wait to become.

Except, here's the thing. I can't become that thing, really. I'm me. If God wanted me to be something else, God would have made me that way. Who am I to tell God that God got it all screwed up anyway? What am I thinking?

Trail Log: Day 43

The Human Trinity
Part Three

TWO DOWN... ONE TO GO. So, if the first part of the Human Trinity is who I wish I wasn't. And the second part is who I'd rather be. Then the third part is the person that I really am. It's not just who I really am. No. It's more than that.

Who I am is my Soul. Not the soul that some people think flies out of your flesh when you die. Not the thing that takes a flier on you when your heart takes a flier on your body. No. Your Embedded Soul. Your Living Soul. For who I really am is *already* given to me by God. From the get-go. Like the label on the package. The one you can't remove. Permanently glued. By God.

And my Soul has five important characteristics. *First*, I'm inherently unique, worthy, and filled with the potential for purpose and meaning by God. In other words, I'm marvelously and wonderfully made by God. *Second*, I am safe. Even when I don't think I am, I really am. Because God has got me no matter what. God has my back and my front. *Third*, I'm unconditionally loved by God. And no one, not even me, can change that. Wow. Unconditional means without fail. Completely trustworthy. Go God! Thanks!

Fourth, I'm wanted and cared for by God. When no one else seems to want me or I don't want myself, God wants me. God's like a care package that keeps on coming. Mail is in. And *fifth*, I am gently held by God. Like a mother who holds her newborn child. Only much more gently. And with an immeasurable desire to stay with me. And hold me.

Gosh, if this is my Soul... who I really am... then that pretty much puts the kibosh on the first two parts of the Human Trinity. I don't need to reject who I am. I don't need to be something else. Why would I? Because, no matter what I'm going through in this canyon of hell right now, I am who I am. I can journey and learn and grow and find my purpose in God, but I don't need to chuck me in the process. Or put on something else. Soulful!

Trail Log: Day 44

Rethinking Theodicy and God

AFTER WALKING AND THINKING and walking and thinking and more thinking yesterday, I guess the idea of the Human Trinity wasn't so great after all. I don't need a Human Trinity. I already have a Human Identity. And a Human Unity. In the person God wanted to create in me in the first place.

With that out of the way, I've re-visited the whole God is powerful, God is good . . . and suffering and evil are real things. And I've come to know that the problem isn't my trying to hold onto all three at the same time. Because I can't. Unless I rethink what they mean.

The biggest one is *Power*. When I started to think about God's power differently, the whole thing got clearer. I had to get off the notion that power means control. That's how we humans define it. The power to make things happen. The power to move mountains. The power to make bad things stop. Or to keep them from happening in the first place. The power to make bad people go away. Or to keep crummy stuff from our back yard. That's *our* definition of power, not necessarily God's.

What if God sees power quite differently? Like power as the power to connect us with God's grace and love when we need it most. Like God as a powerful compass to help us find our way when we're totally lost. Like a powerful friend when we need a powerful but quiet, gentle presence in the midst of our suffering. Like the power to sustain us for one more day when we don't think that we have it in us.

The power of God working in the worst of situations to help hold us up. To help transform our sorrows and loss into a way to tomorrow. The power of new possibilities and options when, just yesterday, there seemed like there were none. The power to keep believing, keep hoping, and keep walking out of this canyon. God is working powerfully within. When I think about God's power in that way, the whole Theodicy mess goes away. That's powerful!

Final Thoughts for This Leg

THANK YOU FOR STAYING with me throughout this past leg, God. I couldn't have made it without you. Honestly, I'm not sure I can say that I've actually made it, though. At least not yet. And I'm feeling pretty powerless in the face of this place. This enormous canyon of my suffering. I admit that I've been leaning a lot on you over the past few days, Lord. And, I'm not totally feeling your power in my life right now. None of my pain feels fair. Not one bit of it. And you're supposed to love me and be the all-powerful one. So, why is this whole mess happening anyway?

I admit that I've blamed you along the way. I've turned you off. I've become more ambivalent about who you really are. And, in the process, I've lost touch with myself. I've spent way too much time trying to be what I'd rather be. Or being ashamed of who I'd rather not be. But seem to be in the end. I've made 'me' the center of my universe. Or the others that I'm trying to emulate.

But, along this leg of the trail, I've learned that loving life begins with loving me. Because you made me, God. And you don't mess around. And I can't love others unless I first love me. I can't love me unless I first let you love me, Lord. I've been getting in my own way, I guess. Sabotaging myself. But that's not what you want for me. And you have the power to help me.

Now, I don't need a celestial magic trick. I don't need you to fix everything in my life. I don't need you to whisk me out of here on some flying carpet. What I ask for is you, Lord. *You* are the source of my power. The power to carry on. To stay open to the future, no matter what. To fuel me forward. To keep the gas tank of my hope as full as possible. To get past my simple notions of you. And to know this: That my heart is what matters most. The one that you gave me in the first place. The one that loves. Never empty. Because you loved me first. And never stop. Powerful. Amen.

Canyon Trail Leg Five:
Violent and Traumatic Suffering

"For dogs are all around me; a company of evildoers encircles me. My hands and feet have shriveled; I can count all my bones. They stare and gloat over me; they divide my clothes among themselves, and for my clothing they cast lots."

PSALM 22: 16–18

Leg Five Canyon Trail Preview

THANKS TO YOU, GOD, I made it safely out of the last trail leg. The remote one with lots of landslides. I couldn't have done it without you. But there appears no let-up to the challenges on this gigantic canyon trail. No easy part. Not a single one. For, just when I could use a break, it's about to get more dangerous.

Apparently, if the landslides don't get you, the wild animals will. The map says that this leg of the trail is a nature preserve. For bears. And leopards. And wolf packs. If I remember my school biology classes, I'm thinking that these animals aren't likely to take kindly to me. I seem to recall that they're all meat eaters. And their preferred menu item is apparently me. That might make me 'dead meat', actually. And the thought of being attacked by these beasts is frightening me, Lord. I can't sleep at night. I can't let down my guard, even a bit. My heart is racing. I'm hyperventilating. I'm sweating bullets. Just the thought of me being maimed by one of these creatures has me freaking out. Totally. Freaking. Out. It's completely traumatic. And traumatizing. Brutal.

God, please protect me from the terrors of this leg. From the violence that I may face. Keep the beasts at bay. And at a distance from me. Set me apart from them and their paths. Don't let them prey on me. Shield me and make me invisible to them. Like a ghost if I cross their way. Then give me back my body and my soul when I'm in the clear. Please protect me, God. Please, don't *you* be invisible. I need you badly. As visible as possible. Thanks, in advance, Lord.

Trail Log: Day 45

Connections Unconnected

Last night wasn't a good night for sleep, I'm afraid. I tossed and turned all night. I kept waking up to the sound of rustling in the bushes near the clearing where I stayed. I had visions of wild coyotes, snakes, wolves, bears, and every other conceivable predator. When I was able to doze off, I dreamed about being physically mauled by all of them at once. I was on the ground, punching and pushing them away. They backed off and then charged at me again. And again. And again. Like waves and torrents of rushing water.

I have to admit that my suffering feels a lot like this sometimes. The connections that I need in my life are torn and frayed and shattered by violence and trauma. I need stable, loving, nurturing connections with others and with God. Of course, I need them for my safety, my nourishment, my comfort, my structure, my affirmation, and my companionship. But I don't need these connections *in reaction to* my fears or pain. Nor in order to achieve anything, really. Nor as a tool to make things happen for me. Nor in order to affirm me or to make me feel better about myself. Nor to relieve my tension or the like.

No. That's not it, I've come to realize. Not at all. Instead, I need healthy, mutually supportive connections with others because I was *inherently created* by God to be in connection. It's like a light bulb or something. When I unplug the cord from the socket in the wall, the light goes out until I plug it back in. That's that. But when the cord gets *yanked* from the socket, the cord gets frayed. The socket gets damaged. The light goes out. Really out. Over and out. And I can't just plug it back in. So the light stays out. And I'm out. . . in the darkness.

If I'm the cord, I feel violated by the abusive, abrupt pull. If I'm the socket, I feel violated by the tearing of my circuits. If I'm the light, I feel violated by the lack of energy. Either way, I'm violated. Violently violated. That's bad.

Trail Log: Day 46

The Violence of Violence

As I was hiking today, I walked past the bones of some rodent. No telling how long it had been there, I suppose. Picked clean. To the bone. I felt bad for the former animal who lived in these bones. It was probably a little thing. Like a chipmunk or ground squirrel. Was probably minding his own business, eating on some grass or weeds. Then Bam. Wham, bang, boom. Overtaken. Gone. Survival of the fittest. Big animals beat up on little animals every time. Hope he didn't suffer too long.

The thoughts of the now-gone little guy had me reflecting on *our* violence against each other. We hit each other. We overpower each other. We injure each other. We kill each other. We've gotten quite good at it, to be honest. We even pay real money to watch people banging the heads of others. Like a prizefight with a guy knocked to the mat. A good car crash. A savage hit on the field. Sometimes *we* also violate others in *real* life.

Sometimes we do it to others sexually. Or emotionally. Or verbally. Or physically. These are action-packed kinds of violence. Some like their violence a bit more subtle. They violate others by their non-action. They neglect others. They withhold from others. They abandon others. They stay with others, but withdraw from them.

However we serve up our violence against others, it hurts them. Big time. Because it draws 'blood'. It leaves scars on others. It dehumanizes and marginalizes them. Not for just a little while. But for a lifetime of suffering by the victims. Real life suffering. Not the fake stuff we see in the movies on the screen. Nope. Real scars. Real blood. Real guts. Real pain. The real deal.

And, along the way, our violence against others makes *us* less human, too. It desensitizes us as the violators. It arrests our own development as human beings, not just that of our victims. And worst of all, it tends to repeat itself. Over and over and over again. Again. And again. . . violently.

Trail Log: Day 47

The Victims are Victimized

Today, I reflected on this whole victim thing. I've spent a lot of time as the victim in my life. Sometimes I've wallowed in it. Had an extended pity party fiesta. "More victim sauce and drinks, please." And maybe some of this is my own fault. I didn't need to stay at the party forever, I guess.

But, sometimes, I didn't want to be a victim and it was thrust upon me. Like, if someone beats up on me, I get abused. I get abused because I get hit. That's that! But that's not only that, as it turns out. People see my bruises and start talking about me behind my back. The whole bruise thing on my face and neck makes people uncomfortable. And curious. And since people like to think the worst, some may blame *me* for this mess. They get the fact that someone put a hurt on me. OK. But then they start to talk amongst themselves. "So, I wonder what she did to deserve that." Or "He must have had it coming to get a beating like that." Or "I should have known it would happen." Like this is all his fault, her fault, and my fault. . . as the victim.

Or even if it's not my fault, somehow I get blamed for not stopping it. The onlookers to my personal train wreck start speculating. Hmm. . .Why didn't I run away? Why didn't I leave? Why didn't I fight back for myself? Why did I stay in that awful situation? Why? Why? Why? And, so it turns out that I'm at fault for my own suffering anyway.

I suffer *once* because someone acted to violate me. I suffer *twice* because I'm blamed for what I did or didn't do. Even if it's not true. Which it's not at all. But who cares about the facts? Truth isn't nearly as much fun as rumors and speculations. Or our worst instincts as human beings. And, finally, I suffer a *third time*. I suffer because the violence against me imprisons me. It creates a new, dark, and sinister lens by which I see the world around me. Trust me, it's not rose colored. And the view is distorted. Askew.

Trail Log: Day 48

The Prisoner Lens

TODAY HAS BEEN REALLY foggy. Hard to see beyond a few feet in front of me. I notice that it throws everything off. Without my usual landmarks, I feel totally lost. Disoriented. I never much thought about how that changes everything. Makes me feel anxious. And that's the point. I never thought much about it. The markers that grounded me and navigated me were simply there. They were working in my sub-conscious to help me—without my having to think about them. Until the fog rolled in. And I got lost.

Violence is a lot like that. The grey and foggy lens distorts my sub-conscious mind. I filter my world through these distortions. And it creates a prison, of sorts, for me. I view the world from within the opaque walls of my prison. One created for me by violence against me. In my prison cell, I can't trust anyone anymore. How could I? Every time I try, I get violated again. And again. Like some crazy wash cycle that keeps spinning me.

It makes it hard to have *any* stable, safe, and loving relationships with others. And when I can't fully trust, I can't fully love. Partly because I'm afraid all the time. But partly because I now hate myself. I've got this thing in my head that I got violated because I actually deserved it. I'm unworthy. Unlovable. I'm bad. To the bone. Bad. Really bad.

And when I hate myself for the whole mess I'm in, I need to earn the respect of myself and of others. I no longer deserve it. I have to earn it back. The hard way. The long way. Go long. Or if I can't earn it, I need to fight for it. Or fight back because I can't ever earn it back. So I bulk up. Do some serious weight training. Build up my stamina. Do aerobics. Two thousand push-ups a day. Five thousand sit-ups. Hit the speed bag for an hour. If only I can get stronger, I can fight back and win. Until I realize that I can't.

So I try to find someone else to fix it. To fix me. To fix him. To fix her. To fix it all.

Trail Log: Day 49

The Lens of Trauma

WHAT MAKES TRAUMA REALLY, really bad is that we never really expect it. Like, I'm walking on this trail. I know that I'm going to get eaten alive later today by bugs. Nasty ones. They bite and bite and bite. And suck my blood. Then make me itch all over. I expect it will happen because it does. Every day. But I never know when. It simply happens to me. Whenever. Randomly, it seems. So I can never really prepare or plan for it.

Trauma is like that, I guess. I'm thinking about what a friend told me a few years ago, "At 6 a.m. this morning, everything was normal in my life. Just like any other day. And then it all ended. I got a call from the hospital that my husband, Mike, was there. In critical condition. Major car crash. I needed to get there. S.T.A.T. It was never normal again. My life changed forever in that instant. Never the same again."

Trauma is traumatic. I can't ever really be ready for it. Everything that connects me is *suddenly* disengaged. My anxiety level shoots up. To the sky, actually. Or maybe to the moon. Or Mars. All my normal coping skills hit the skids. The things that help to hold me up are ripped up from under me. Suddenly. Violently. And there's nothing to replace them in the moment.

What's worse, all the dysfunctions of my life and my relationships suddenly get worse. Exacerbated. What was once not great just got strained to the breaking point now.

And I can't think straight. I've got ten thousand emotions swirling around in my head and heart. I can't understand things. I can't remember things. I can't make any sense of things. My hearing is suddenly selective. I remember only a few words. And I seize on them. And interpret them in worst case, irrational ways sometimes. All the normal noise in the system suddenly becomes a blaring horn. All the normal lights become blinding spotlights. I'm now a deer in the headlight. With tunnel vision. So I freeze. Or run.

Trail Log: Day 50

Processing Violence and Trauma

As I walked the trail today, I couldn't help but continue to reflect on the story of my friend. The one who lost her husband, Mike, in that terrible car crash a few years ago. It was an incredibly tough time for her after Mike died. I remembered how traumatic and violent it all felt. And I remember how jumbled up she said it all became in the months that followed.

And I remember my own suffering. Some of it violent in its own way, I guess. And how jumbled up my own feelings got. Like popcorn in a bag cooking in the microwave. Kernels flying everywhere. But they're in the bag, so I can't see them clearly. I hear them. Can't really 'see' them. But I know that stuff is getting flung around in the bag. Maybe that's what violent suffering is like. A bag of popcorn getting nuked in my microwave. I try to process it, but I can't really. Things are popping.

Sometimes the pain is immediate. It's in my face. Literally. In my tears. Right now. . . But sometimes the pain comes out of nowhere. I'm chugging along as well as I can. All of a sudden, it hits me. I have no idea why. But it hits me hard. Like a tidal wave of grief and pain. No one understands what's going on with me. I've become unpredictable. . .

But sometimes my pain comes in waves. Not sudden tidal waves. Not the tsunami type out of nowhere. Rather, the wave after wave of grief and sorrow and pain. Like the steady pounding of the ocean during a storm. One after another. Pounding. On me. At times, the waves abate for a while. And then I see something that reminds me of my pain or loss. And a big wave crashes in on me. Like some trigger got pulled. Just for me. . .

The worst pain, though, is the diffused, chronic, and generalized pain that I feel. Like some ill-defined, vague malaise. It's got me in a daily funk. And I don't mean a song or dance. However the pain manifests itself, though, violence and trauma break *all* the rules. Popcorn getting nuked.

Trail Log: Day 51

A Mother God

TODAY, I GOT UP early to watch the sunrise. And I ended the day watching the sunset. Beautiful. Invigorating. Relaxing. Rejuvenating. Restful. Peaceful. Wonderful.

Especially against the harsh, barren backdrop of this canyon I'm in. The rocks carve sharp, hard lines on the horizon. The sheer magnitude of it can almost feel traumatic at times. The wind and snow and sheets of rain can lash at me violently in this place. But the rising and setting of the sun softens everything. Adds color and texture. And they're dependable. The sun rises and sets. Each and every day. Of my life. Like clockwork.

Perhaps God is a lot like that for me. Even in the midst of my trauma and violent pain in this place, God is there. Dependable. Like clockwork. God provides me with a sense of security. Of proximity. Of love. In some ways, God is like a loving mother. Who carries me in her womb. Who nurtures me within her own body. Carries me. Feeds me. Helps me to grow and develop. I'm like a child at the center of my mother's universe. Of God's.

And like any good mother, it's not that I'm simply held. It's rather 'how' I'm held. God holds me firmly but gently. Whenever I want or need to be held. And God's eyes aren't ever tired or bloodshot as God looks upon me. God's eyes are those of an adoring mother. Never estranged. Never preoccupied. Never late or out of the room. Always there. Just in time.

And God's eyes don't just look upon me with love. God's eyes truly affirm me. Truly mirror my own amazement and wonder. God's eyes cry with mine when I suffer violence or trauma. God's hands gently wipe away my tears.

So, what if I saw God as not just a Father? But *also* a Mother. Who births me, who holds me, who rocks me to sleep, who sings to me, who reads to me, who guides me, and who loves me unconditionally. Like only a mother can. Mother God. Ms. Giver and Sustainer God. Thank you, Mom.

Trail Log: Day 52

God in Trauma and Violence

I'M NEARING THE END of this trail leg now. Might finish it later today or early tomorrow if all goes well. I may not, as I've come to understand in this canyon each day. There's a lot of stuff that's simply out of my control. Violent weather. Oppressive heat and cold. Nasty, powerful dust storms. Crippling fog. Torrential rain. Heavy winds in my face. But I'll make it, I think. I've gotten this far by God's strength, peace, grace, and presence.

God is greater than all the violence and trauma around me. God is like my best friend in all of this. God is here. God speaks encouragement to me in a softness that only God can have. God is close by. So God can hear me. My prayers. My cries. My appeals. My laments. My words. Even when I don't have the strength to speak, God hears my thoughts.

When things speed up and get chaotic, God is like a friend who slows things down. Slows me down. Gets me to breathe more fully and slowly. And God gets on my eye level. Doesn't stand over me. But sits with me. Right there. And God helps me to reflect by helping me stay in the 'now'. God keeps me from getting stuck in the past. Or on the future. From fixating on the worst possible. Or the most unrealistic. Rather, keeps me in the present moment.

Not just that, but God helps remind me of something: That I have gotten through bad, traumatic things before. God has helped me *in* them. God is *in* them right now. God is working *in* them. With me. Like a friend. A true blue friend.

Lastly, God is helping me to reframe where I am in my violent pain. In my trauma. God is planting seeds within me. Seeds of transformation. So I'll not only get through this. I'll somehow come out whole. Maybe different. But whole. I may not know it now, but I will someday. For when the forces of trauma and violence overtake me, God overtakes them. God takes them and weaves them into something new. Special. For me.

Final Thoughts for This Leg

Thank you, God, for getting me this far. This whole thing has been traumatic. The suddenness and the magnitude of my pain have been unsettling. Unnerving, actually. Along the way, I've felt like all my moorings have been cut. I'm adrift in a turbulent sea. A sandstorm, to be more exact. For I'm in this vast and desolate canyon. The sheer size of this place violates my sense of me. I'm being swallowed up in its enormity. I'm being pummeled by the wind, the rain, the sun, the cold, the heat, and the force of nature. From every turn, I'm hit. It hurts, to be honest. And it feels like my troubles are piling on. Like compounding interest. But not in a good way. It all comes at me so fast, too. Too fast to process. It's like every day is the 'new' worst day of my life. That must be the definition of 'trauma'. Of violence. Against me, Lord.

But I've come to know one thing from this past leg of my walk: Today is passing. This moment is passing. My pain and suffering are passing. Even when I don't feel that way. As I empty my pain through my prayers with you, through the tears that I shed, and through my cries and anguish, you hear me. And you don't just 'hold' stuff for me. You take stuff into yourself. And, as you do, you give me new birth, Lord. You breathe your love and grace into me. You continue to form me from the dirt of the earth. You mold me. You create me anew each day. I have no idea where this is going, God. But you are creating something special in this place, in this time, and in this space.

There is no place out of your loving reach, God. I need to trust you. I need to have faith in you. Sometimes I need to slow down. I even need to get out of your way and mine at times. For I know that you are working. It's a work zone. Right here in the canyon. Amen.

Canyon Trail Leg Six:
Supporting the Longer-Term Needs of Suffering: Spirituality

"The Lord is my chosen portion and my cup; you hold my lot. The boundary lines have fallen for me in pleasant places; I have a goodly heritage. I bless the Lord who gives me counsel; in the night also my heart instructs me. I keep the Lord always before me; because he is at my right hand, I shall not be moved. Therefore my heart is glad, and my soul rejoices; my body also rests secure."

PSALM 16: 5–9

Leg Six Canyon Trail Preview

I SO APPRECIATE YOUR getting me to this point, Lord. I've now made it past the worst legs of the canyon, I think. I've survived the landslides and the wild, ravenous animals. And I get this remote sense in me that I'm now closer to the end than to the beginning. That gives me hope. It fills me with good feelings.

But the way ahead is not an easy one, to be sure. Lots of challenges yet to come. For, according to the trail map, this next leg is sneaky hard. On the surface, the trail is fairly flat and wide. Pretty well marked. So far, so good. But here's the catch: There are spots of deep and sticky mud. Areas of quick sand. And some hidden, yet massive potholes along the way, too. Lots of mud, muck, mire, and crevices at nearly every step. Where you sink slowly and deeply. Into the deep and dark abyss. And there's no one else here to lend a hand. To extend their arms. To throw me a line. To pull me out. If I fall in, I'm likely never to get out. I'll stay there. Perhaps forever. Sunk. Covered up. Lost. Gone.

Lord, keep my feet on solid ground here. Keep me out of the pits. Out of the pain and despair here. Don't let me drown in the quick sand of my suffering and my pain. Don't let me be buried in my grief and loss and sorrow. Keep my head above it all. Keep me breathing. Please keep me on this side of the ground. On steady ground. Firm ground. Settled ground. Please keep me fully grounded. In you. And in your way. Let me follow your trail. Around the potholes of this trail leg. Lord, keep me safe. Keep me connected to your strong arms. Physically, spiritually, and otherwise. Thanks, in advance, God.

Trail Log: Day 53

Spirituality Defined

I THINK I HAVE the end in sight now. Finally. After days and days of walking and fretting and wondering. After days of aching feet and legs. I may be closer to my way out of here. I find that, with my exit from the canyon now within view, I feel up to thinking about the bigger picture for a change. Funny thing. It's not until I feel that I may yet make it that I finally take time to feel it. And, today, I feel at one with everything about me, to be honest. I feel connected somehow to all things. Heck, even to *me* for that matter. Wow.

Maybe, that's what Spirituality is all about. Connectedness. When I feel Spiritual, I feel joined up. Connected. Aligned. Together. Like pieces of a puzzle that were made to fit together nicely. So, as I was walking today, I reflected on my Spirituality. Who and what am I connected with?

I thought about God. When I feel Spiritual, I feel connected to God as my higher power. I feel connected to everything that God has created in this world—even this canyon, if you can believe it. And because I feel connected to God and all creation, I feel connected to me. For, if God loves me, I need to love myself, too.

Then, because I feel connected with God and myself, I can feel connected with others. I don't run into a lot of others in this canyon. At least people-wise. But I wish I had others here with me. I remember when I did. I will again someday soon. I need others in my life. And they need me. Communion. With others.

So, when I'm connected with God, and me, and others, I can also connect with my purpose and meaning in my life. Not my daily goals or to-do lists. Rather, the things that matter at a deeper level. Like why I'm alive in the first place.

Lastly, I'm connected with my gifts and talents. The things that God gave me in order to put my connectedness into action. The 'just do it' stuff. So. . . God, me, my purpose, and my gifts and talents. All joined up. Yep. Spiritual Super Glue.

Trail Log: Day 54

The Trap of Religiosity

SO, I WAS REALLY getting into the Spirituality stuff yesterday while I walked. I was feeling good. A little skip to my step. Humming a tune. Doing fine. Like walking on a cloud.

And I asked myself this: Where does my *religion* fit into the whole thing? Is this a part of my Spirituality? Does it have to be? Can I have one without the other? That one is a big one, for sure. There are times when I feel religious, but not Spiritual. And times when I feel Spiritual, but not religious. I like to read the Bible. I like church. I like sacraments.

I like ritual. I like structure. I like worshiping with others. I like sermons. I like coffee hour after worship. I like the donuts and cookies, as well, if you catch my drift. So I figure that having a religious tradition is just fine. It's a place I can call my faith 'home' of sorts. It's a place I can set down some roots. Be with others. Support others. Pray with others. Pray for others with others. Have Spiritual time with others. With family. Friends.

But I've come to know that I need more than religion. For no one faith tradition captures all truth all the time and for all places. No one church defines 'the answer'. No one faith is perfect, and none has the final word. God does. I need to remember that. Really.

In fact, when I get too 'religious', I can get too rigid. Stuck. Not stretched. I defend my turf rather than welcoming others in. I stop asking questions. In truth, I get lazy. And I get only part of the picture. Like a half-finished work of art. For God is the artist. God doesn't live within the four walls of any church. Nor does God sleep each night under a steeple. God has spoken, to be sure, but is still speaking. No one book or place or thing can constrain God, define God, command God, invoke God, consume God, or be God.

So, I need to be Spiritual, really, before I can be religious in any meaningful, completed sense of the word. If I stop at simply being religious, I may have simply 'stopped'. Being.

Trail Log: Day 55

The Spiritual Whole

Part One

I STOPPED DURING THE heat of today under a beautiful tree. There aren't a lot of these in the canyon. This tree was near a streambed, mixed in amidst some scrub and other growth. I found a nice, dry spot beneath the tree. Because this was such an anomaly, I started to reflect on the tree for some reason. Maybe bored today. Maybe philosophical. Maybe I simply got Spiritual.

And I'm thinking that this tree has a lot of parts to it. The leaves, the branches, the trunk, the bark, and the roots. The part that I can't actually see is really the most important: The roots. The things that draw in the water from the stream to nourish the tree. Hmm. Or maybe the leaves, which I can see. They take in the sunlight and also nourish the tree. Or maybe the trunk, which keeps the tree straight and strong. Then I realized that I'd been losing the forest for the trees with all this 'parts' stuff.

When I do that, I make the 'whole' lesser than the sum of the parts. Maybe that's true with my Spirituality too. When I make the parts matter most, I become disembodied. It's like I start dissecting myself into small pieces on a paper plate or something. When I do that, I reduce myself to my gifts or qualities or behaviors. Or even worse, to my results or my outcomes. Like I can be seen as something that can be measured. By others. Or myself, even. Or I become simply my efforts, even when they fail. Or worse, yet, I become the parts of my disease and suffering. My symptoms. My fever. My cough. My test results. My prognosis. My life expectancy. My medical chart data points.

When the whole of me is lesser than the sum of my parts, I become disconnected and disembodied. Like pieces of glass or pottery strewn on the floor. Seen as something to be swept up with a dustpan. Or like pieces of a puzzle where a few of the pieces are missing. Really messes up the puzzle, doesn't it? Because you can't complete it.

We're not pieces. We're the puzzle.

Trail Log: Day 56

The Spiritual Whole
Part Two

Today, I continued to muse on the puzzle pieces thing. It's like a song that you can't get out of your mind. I think I even dreamed about puzzles last night. They were dancing around me, singing some puzzle song. Whoa. I'm getting way too into this.

But, as I walked today, I couldn't help myself. And I went back to thinking about the whole and the parts. I've now realized what 'the whole of me is lesser than the sum of my parts' means. Bad news. I don't want to be a bunch of pieces. So, what if the whole of me is not lesser than, but equal to, the sum of my parts. That should do it!

Ah. . . maybe not. What's wrong with being simply a whole? All my parts equal me. My whole me. It's wrong because being only 'whole' can make me an object or a thing. Perhaps better than a set of puzzle pieces which don't quite add up to the whole puzzle. But it makes me only the 'completed' puzzle. Something that can be observed. Critiqued. It makes me static. Finished. Done. And that makes me limited to what I *already* am.

Frankly, it makes me a zero-sum game. Like a statue, fixed in stone, forevermore. Everlasting, dude. And this makes me less than human. Dehumanized, actually. And I don't want to be a statue. I want to be a person. A fully embodied person with a body, mind, and my very soul. It's not enough to be only embodied. I need to be fully embodied. Fully connected. Fully alive. Fully transforming and growing. A finished puzzle or statue or painting isn't fully anything except fully done. I'm not done. I'm not ready for somebody to take me out of the oven and put a fork in me. I'm still cooking.

In fact, I'm not even cooking yet. I'm being marinated in a special sauce. It's God's special sauce. All this is to say that the whole of me can't be simply the sum of my parts.

My parts do matter. My whole self does matter. But God has even bigger plans for me.

Trail Log: Day 57

The Spiritual Whole
Part Three

Do you believe it? I awoke last night from a seemingly sound sleep. I was dreaming about the puzzle pieces again. I've got to stop drinking so much stream water before I go to bed. Last night, I had this nightmare about the puzzle. The pieces were taunting the whole. The whole was taunting the pieces. Everybody was fighting with everybody else. Not pretty when puzzle pieces fight.

But it occurred to me that they might be fighting each other out of fear. It was like each side of this puzzle scrum was scared. A Spiritual Panic Attack, maybe. Because they knew that neither had the answer to true Spirituality. Like they were holding on for dear life while hanging from some puzzle canyon rock high above the canyon floor. They were probably screaming to themselves in fright, "Hold on. Hang on." And the other side was telling themselves, "Make a circle. Form a line. Protect our flanks. Steady, boys."

What were they all so scared of? Perhaps they knew that, in truth, the whole is more than the sum of its parts. More. Much more. Spiritually much more. For we were made by God to become even more. Even more. No limits. Not those that we impose on ourselves. Or others impose on us. God made us not to cut us into puzzle pieces. Not to create some statue. No. God created us as linked up pieces— making us living, breathing art. Unfinished art. Because we're always making it along the way.

God wants us to actualize our very being by not ever really fully actualizing it. Instead, we're always 'on the way'. And we do more than simply actualize. We seek out and find God as we walk and stretch and grow and learn. In the process, we keep making something new. Over and over and over again. In us and with others as we go. Like an artist's colony. Something like that. Perhaps not even God knows what we'll all become in this community of Spirituality. But God believes in us. That's all we need.

Trail Log: Day 58

Levels of Spirituality

I FINALLY GOT THE puzzle pieces thing out of my head. Thankfully. And I've settled on this: That my Spiritual *'whole'* is greater than the sum of my Spiritual parts. I need all my parts. And the whole matters. But I'm not finished yet. I'm, therefore, more than my parts or even my whole. So, I'm thinking about me as evolving, stretching, and growing.

I'm also reflecting on my life to-date. Yeah, I've faced a lot of pain and suffering and loss. Heck, I'm in this canyon, in case you forgot the story line here. But, in the midst of my suffering, what is it that I focus on each day? I realized that I focus most of me on me, to be honest. Not me as Spiritual me. But the Unconscious 'me', meaning the things I need to keep me going. Like filling up the tank at a gas station. Like stopping at the drive-through for dinner on the go. Yeah, the fast food stuff. Tastes good. Real good. But real bad for me. And I focus on all my unconscious impulses. You know, the getting angry stuff. The fight or flight stuff when I'm afraid. All that stuff.

While all the 'me' stuff matters, I need to focus on more than that. I need to also focus on what everyone else tells me are the 'rules' of my life, the Semi-Conscious 'me'. I'm talking about the norms, expectations, limits, and learning that everyone else impose on me. All that I have to believe because *they* believe it. Because someone else told them that it's the only way to believe. Pass it on, brother. Sister. Semi-Consciously, please. Just under the radar.

But hold on now... I need to focus *most of all* on the Spiritual, Fully-Conscious 'me'. The real best me. The whole, integrated, fully feeling, totally conscious me. In this moment. With a focus on growing me Spiritually beyond my fragmented, disembodied life. Growing me more fully into a vibrant, God/Other-connected and Spiritual person who lives in the space of Fully-Conscious choices. Even when I suffer pain and loss.

Trail Log: Day 59

Spiritual Practices
The Sacred One

TODAY ON THE TRAIL, I looked at the sky. I was struck by its deep blue color. More so by the billowy white clouds that painted a brilliant contrast against it. And I wondered. How hard must God work to splash the sky's canvas with such amazing clouds? Then it came to me. Not that hard. Anymore. For God's been at it since time began. God's had lots and lots of practice.

Some days, God paints just a few. Like the sprinkling of stardust on a sprawling piece of art. On other days, God blankets the sky with cloud after cloud. Some days, they're white. Some days, grey or even black. Some days, God takes the day off from this painting stuff. Tends to other things, I guess. Leaves the sky a simple blue. God's got this sacred thing down, though. Lots of practice, I guess.

And what about me? My Spirituality. How much practice do I have in this space? If I'm honest, not much. So I've decided that I need to work at it with more discipline each day. And my Spirituality has to start with the Divine One: God. God is the author and creator of all things, living and otherwise. All things are therefore sacred in God's eyes. Yes, even the rocks. The weeds. The spiders. The roaches. Yes, even the rats. Yuk, but yes. And if they are sacred and of God, they have inherent worth and beauty.

And it's not just things that are sacred. Every day of every week of every year is sacred. Not just the Sabbath. Every day. In fact, every second and minute and hour. For all time is sacred and of God. And, by the way, it's not just us, and things, and time. It's everything we say or do.

Every act, word, and intention are sacred, because they are meant to honor God. We honor God when we say or do or even think with hearts of gratitude. Even when we have every right to say otherwise. And are not in the mood to embrace the Mystery. Like when we suffer. That's why they call it faith, I guess. But trust me, God's got it. God will make it work. Book it.

Trail Log: Day 60

Spiritual Practices

Creation

I HAVE TO ADMIT that I'm having some problems with thinking about rocks and weeds and mice as 'sacred'. I may have to work on that one for a while. Might take some real practice and discipline on my part. But when I begin to see all things as part of creation and not some cosmic mistake like poison ivy, I see my own place in things more clearly. I begin to see the enormity and complexity of everything around me. Everything looks bigger and more expansive. Everything seems more connected and joined up. I start to feel smaller in the midst of it all.

At first, this kind of scared me, to be frank. It's easier when I think I'm the King of the Heap. The Queen of the Sand Pile. The 'Grand Poopaah' of all things. The world is my platter. My snack tray. My juice bottle. My kingdom and castle. But when I let that go a bit and scale 'me' down, it lightens me up. I'm not responsible for everything. I am not lord of it all. I am simply part of it all. That's a relief. And when I'm only part of it all, I look at it all differently.

Spirituality means that I respect Creation. I live in harmony with it. By reciprocity. This means that I try to restore what I remove. I'm careful about what I use. But when I need to, I try to make it whole somehow. And I say "thank you" to God for its use. I'm thankful because I have no inherent right to Creation. It's a gift. Freely given. But a gift, nonetheless. When I receive these gifts, I do so with humility and gratitude. And I share them with others. Because community matters just as much as individuality.

This means that creation is not 'dog eat dog'. Not even 'dog bite dog'. Not even a nibble. How about a kiss, instead? A kiss of interdependent, loving, caring, sharing mutuality. I share because it's the right thing to do. But also for this reason: I need others to share creation with me too. Especially when I'm sick or broke or broken-up or heart-broken or simply broken.

Trail Log: Day 61

Spiritual Practices
Belonging

As I walk this leg of the trail each day, my shoes gather dirt inside of them. The dirt gets into my socks and the bottom of my pants. Sometimes, I can brush it off. Sometimes, it stains things. Turns them brown or tan or even orange. A nuisance, to be sure. But the dirt and dust remind me that I am rooted to the earth and soil. The land.

The land is life-giving, life-sustaining, life-orienting, and life-receiving in the end. I look to the land for markers in my walk. As milestones reached. As places yet to reach. I belong to this canyon place, even though I'm trying hard to walk out of it in the end. While it's hard to look at the soil as sacred, it is. It is a part of me. And 'I' of 'it'. We belong to each other. It sustains and holds me. Not just me, actually. This land, this soil, this earth holds us all. *Together.* We belong to this place we call earth, our home.

And we belong to each other. We were meant to breathe and talk and sing and cry and joyfully shout with others, not alone. In a circle, actually. The earth is a circle of sorts. So are we. The only way we can truly see each other clearly is to stand in a circle. That means in the round. Not on top of each other. Or in front of others. Or behind others. Not in domination over others. Not from the rooftop overlooking others. But in a circle. A circle of life. A circle that sees each other, shares with each other, and lifts each other when they're down. A circle that protects each other. So we don't lose circle members. A circle that loves each other. So we don't let others down.

This circle isn't a game of musical chairs. There are chairs for everyone. In a real circle. A big and diverse circle. Where every chair and person matter. All grounded in this place we call home. Rooted firmly here and now. In the sacred earth. The sacred soil. The sacred ground. Rooted deeply. In the place where we were made to live. Together. Rooted forever right here. In the place where we belong. That's Spiritual.

Trail Log: Day 62

Spiritual Practices

Silence

YESTERDAY WAS AN AMAZING day. The usual clatter of the wind and water and birds went suddenly still as I walked into a valley. It was initially a little weird. I'm used to the noise around me to keep me company as I walk. It reminds me that I'm not alone. There's life around and about me. I'm a part of things. The sound of my feet on the ground blends nicely with the sounds of nature. Like a small orchestra, I'm thinking. Or the sound of my humming blends seamlessly with the chirps of birds. Or the sound of my cries blends morosely with the howls of the coyotes at night. Sometimes, I don't even hear the sounds anymore. Even though they're there.

But then today, as I said, everything went quiet. Suddenly, it seems. After I moved past the weirdness of it all, I began to like it. It took my breath away, actually. In a good way. I stopped in my tracks and simply took it all in. The silence. Wasn't sure that I could actually take silence in. But I did. Amazing stuff. I was listening to silence. Think about it. Listening to the sound of silence. Silent Wow!

Without the noise, I became more mindful of the moment. This very moment. I discovered the power of contemplation. Of simple reflection. Of knowing something special without having to understand it. Knowing the inherent wisdom of silence without taking any notes. Wisdom so deep that it transcends everything I thought I knew before.

Oh, and I discovered something else in the silence. I began using *all* five of my senses to sense the silence fully. Really. I could see the silence. Feel the silence. Hear the silence. Touch the silence. And taste the silence. All my senses at once. In unison. Delicious.

So it seems like everything I thought about silence was wrong. It's not scary or empty after all. It's not a punishment. Or part of my awful suffering. No. It's a life-giving, grace-filled gift. It's a friendly companion that I plan to pack for the trip more often.

Trail Log: Day 63
Spiritual Practices
Simplicity

I'VE GOT TO BE honest with you right now. My clothes are starting to tatter. I have only so many changes of outfits out here. I can't carry a whole wardrobe on my back. There weren't any mules for hire when I started on this journey of suffering. Washing my clothes in the stream is all well and good. But rubbing my stuff on the rocks to get the dirt out wears my clothes out. I'm worn out. So are my clothes. And my shoes. I don't even try to wash them. Afraid the leather will come apart. The dirt's probably holding the soles onto my boots, if I'm honest. Leave well enough alone. No one else smells my feet.

You might say that I live in 'poverty'. I don't have much at all. I'm poor in every sense of the word. I live day-to-day, sometimes minute-to-minute. Or, at least it feels that way. And it's no way to live. I deserve better. And so does everyone else who experiences pain, poverty, hunger, and the lack of basics. Especially in the face of their suffering.

Sometimes, I hear that being Spiritual means that we should live simply. Simple is not the same as poverty. Simplicity means that we live simply. We focus our lives on 'being' rather than over-complicating, accumulating, consuming, possessing, achieving, and holding onto it all when we've 'arrived'. Simplicity is living for *this* moment rather than for tomorrow or the next day or someday somewhere down the road called 'Something'.

When we live simply, the beauty of ordinary, everyday things in life jumps out at us. As special. And beautiful. Simply unique and amazing. Simply put. The little things are joyful. Because they're so simple, this joy is free. It's independent. Of our wealth, our accomplishments, our stuff, or someone else's stuff. Anybody's stuff for that matter.

Most of all, living simply helps us to focus on the one true thing: God. The Divine One. The Sacred One. The Spiritual One. Number One. The One who deserves First Place.

Trail Log: Day 64

Spiritual Practices

Honor

TODAY, THE SKIES GOT dark. Very dark. Never seen them so dark since I've been in this canyon. So dark that I thought even the sky is suffering. Not just me for a change. Not just a little head cold kind of suffering. Rather, a full-blown migraine headache in the clouds. Then the wind went quiet for a second. Just a second. Until it blew again with a fury. And the skies emptied torrential rain. Blowing, biting rain. That seemed to cut my face. Cut through my clothes. Like scissors cutting through thin paper. I wanted to cut and run. But I didn't. Scared, but I didn't cut and run. I got under a ledge and waited it out.

I was proud of myself in all of this. I have every reason to go to pieces these days. At the drop of a hat. Or a raindrop. I'm sick and I'm tired. Sick and tired of it all. But I'm also Spiritual. It's in my nature. I'm Spiritually 'wired' to show courage in the face of my fears. . . in the teeth of those things that scare me. I can face the wind and the rain if I have to. Or take shelter briefly to fight another day. Rest up, then get back after it soon.

I'm not only courageous, but I'm capable of self-control in the face of setbacks or trouble. I don't have to react to everything that blows in my face. I can step back, look at it more objectively, and decide what to do. Do what's in my own best interest. Not as a default response to some external stimuli. I'm not a mouse on a wheel. I'm Spiritual.

And I have inherent integrity as a person. This means that I can stand aligned. With myself, my values, my bigger purpose, my meaning, my faith, and my beliefs. I can be true to myself. I can also be true to others. True to my word to them. True to the idea of fairness toward them. Justice for them. True to protecting their rights. Good cause.

It's all inside of me already. But it takes courage and practice to hone these things. I just need to use them with honor. God has honored me by making me. Back at you, God.

Trail Log: Day 65

Spiritual Practices

Seasons of Life

IT SEEMS LIKE I'VE been in this canyon forever. I know I haven't. But sometimes it seems like it. Like time compressed into a bottle. All four seasons, to be exact. Here, I can feel *all* the seasons within a few days or so. It can go from brutally cold to brutally hot. From icy to steamy. From parched to soaked. From dry to humid. From sunny to cloudy. Not the stuff of vacation postcards, I suppose. "Wish you were here. Not." Not sending it.

But, in the moments of sacred silence and reflection, I've concluded that our lives have seasons too. Like the weather, but different. For the seasons of my life are not always neat. They don't run in regular cycles. Spring doesn't always follow winter. Sometimes summer follows fall. Sometimes winter seems to go on forever. Then I get a day of summer. Then back to winter. Then quickly over to fall. All mixed up. But seasons nonetheless.

And, as a Spiritual being, I need to practice 'being' in them as they come and go. I need to enter into winter: A time of rest, reflection, meditation, and solitude. Or time with others. Step back. Slow down. Go inside. Build a fire. Stay warm. Stay dry.

But I need to welcome spring, as well: A time of new possibilities. Hope. The germination of new seeds. Rapid growth. Stuff breaking forth from the ground.

Summer: My time for vitality and activity. Enjoyment. Energy. Striving. Completing. It's a time for goals and causes, with breaks for sunshine, rest, and lively fellowship.

And then there's fall: A time for gathering what I've sown. To prepare. Store things up. To gather together with others to give thanks. To celebrate. To look back. To remember. And to let go. Like the leaves on a tree. They need to let go. The leaves are finite. So am I. So I need to let go sometimes, as well. It's hard, but I need to try.

Everything is Spiritual. If I make it so. What's more, everything is seasonal. If I let it be so.

Final Thoughts for This Leg

THANK YOU, LORD, ONCE again for leading me forward on this trail. For helping me out of this canyon of pain and loss. I've felt more connected on this leg of my journey. Actually connected. I've paid more attention to where I fit in the universe of this place. And I've felt more whole as a result. I've come to understand that I am not simply a bunch of parts that work together. And that my 'whole' is worth far more than the sum of my parts. For I am special and unique in your eyes. When I get hung up on all the rules I'm supposed to follow, the connectedness frays a bit. To be sure, I need to believe in something. I do need some structure. But, when I 'marry' that structure, I get estranged from you, God. And that's not good. For you aren't limited to one Book or one set of rules. You aren't defined by dogma or sacraments or rites or rituals.

I need to spend more time with you. The mysterious one. Who cannot be constrained. I need to see you more fully in all things, both living and not. For you created it all, anyway. I need to see this place, even this canyon, as sacred space. I need to feel a greater belonging. A part of something far greater than me alone. I need to belong with other people, my community of faith, my place of work, my friends, and my family. Truly belong. And when I get out of here someday soon, I need to sometimes simply sit. With you. In silence. Silence is uncomfortable, God. But I need more of it. With you. To just sit together.

In so doing, I can slow down my life. Live my life more simply. Focus on honoring you, even as I honor myself more. And live my life in the knowledge that all life has its seasons. Nothing is permanent. Except you. And everything that's within you. If I feel that more fully, God, I can live with the changes all around me. Without fear. Because I'm with you. You, Lord, who knows no single season. You are our God for all seasons. Amen.

Canyon Trail Leg Seven:
Supporting the Immediate Needs of Suffering

"The Lord is my shepherd, I shall not want. He makes me lie down in green pastures; he leads me besides still waters; he restores my soul. He leads me in right paths for his name's sake."

PSALM 23: 1–3

Leg Seven Canyon Trail Preview

THIS TRAIL IS REALLY starting to wear on me, Lord. The canyon goes on and on and on. Seemingly forever. Forget the 'seemingly' part. Let's go with simply forever. On this next leg of the trail, my biggest challenge is weariness. The accumulation of the elements. The weather. The monotony. The daily grind of it all. The wear and tear of it all. My clothes are wearing fast. They're wearing thin in spots. They're full of holes. And I don't mean 'holy', God. I wish it were. And my feet ache a lot these days. When I pull my boots off each night, the blisters on my feet hurt. They're red and inflamed. My bones ache and wake me in the night with pain. And in the morning, I feel stiff in my joints. Feel like I got 'stiffed' while I slept.

Overall, I feel beaten up. I need someone to care for me. And meet *my* needs. But the last time that I checked, I was completely alone. The cavalry is not coming, I'm afraid. No reinforcements are on the way. Except you, God. Please meet me where I am here. Please attend to my wounds. Please attend to my tired body. Please attend to my weary soul. Please welcome me when no one else will.

Please quench my thirst when I'm parched. Keep the water running, if you could. Please feed me when I'm too tired to do it myself. Please give me peace and rest as I sleep. Please lie down beside me and gently close my eyes each night in your mercies and grace. Please be there for me and keep me going. Keep me coping. Or simply keep me. Thanks, in advance, God.

Trail Log: Day 66

Coping Pitfalls
Maladaptive Ones

WHEN I WAS ON the trail yesterday, I ran across this beetle-looking thing. It was big and ugly. Lots of legs under some mean armor jacket. I was tempted to put my boot on it, but I got to reflecting on the Spirituality thoughts I've had recently. Then I thought 'live and let live' and quit walking. But I felt like doing more. So I grabbed a stick and pushed the bug to the side of the path. So it wouldn't get stepped on by someone else.

But, here's the thing. The beetle headed right back onto the path. What is this guy thinking? Try to do something nice for this ugly thing. And he walks back into traffic. The more I thought about it, the more I saw myself as this beetle. Maybe the bug was in denial. Maybe he was 'acting out' in some form of protest against my help. Maybe he was trying to be some kind of hero or something. You know, defy the odds. Against all odds. Or maybe he was a 'victim' or martyr. You know, the 'I'm not worthy' kind of thing. The 'woe is me' kind of thing. Who knows in the end? I couldn't ask him. He's a beetle. They don't talk.

Sometimes, though, I act like a beetle in my suffering. I do the same things in my efforts to cope. I do the same things that have barely worked for me in the past. But I do so in the face of the *new* realities of my suffering. Doing the same thing, while expecting a different outcome. It's bad enough when things are going well. But it's *completely maladaptive* in the face of suffering, pain, and loss— especially sudden and traumatic situations. Like mine, if I'm honest.

What's worse, in the midst of my new suffering contingencies, my current coping mechanisms, however faulty, are kicked right out from under me. What seemed to marginally work for me in the past no longer does. The situation has now changed big-time... but I can't change in response to it. So I return to the path. Just like the beetle did. Even though it's a bad idea. Over and over again.

Trail Log: Day 67

Coping Pitfalls

Keep It Running

I CONTINUE TO REFLECT on my beetle tendencies in the midst of my suffering. I see a lot of him in me. I'm a lot like him, I guess. But the beetle doesn't fully describe me. I'm more than that! I cope like a big run-away train, I've concluded. Like this giant locomotive and train cars out of control on some remote set of tracks somewhere in the middle of nowhere. Like in this canyon of pain. And I'm the train engineer of this mess on wheels.

Now, let's pretend that my suffering is the train. I'm going to derail and wreck completely unless I do something to prevent it. And do it fast. So, what do I do in the context of my own pain and loss? What I've done in the past is to *keep the train running*. If only I can keep this thing going, someone will come to rescue me. Just keep it going. Don't stop. Heck, sometimes I've tried to speed the train up. Who knew? Who in their right mind would? But *I* have. Like if I speed it up, the 'yuk' will go away faster. Yeah. Right. And how about the times when I've tried to repair the tracks in front of me? Just stay ahead of the game. Keep repairing. Just in time. Ah, and the best idea is to lay more track in front of me. If I only lay more, I'll never run out of track. And the train won't derail. Except that I can't lay it fast enough. Crash. Boom. Disaster. Me. Bad.

Sometimes the best thing to do is to simply *stop* the train. Take a break. Step back. Assess it all with a clearer head. Resist the 'either-or' thing. Look at options. Adopt the 'optimal' thing. With more facts in hand. Having asked more questions. Sometimes, in the midst of my suffering, I've needed to do that a lot more. I've needed to give up the wheel. Let go of the illusion of control. Slow down and think. In order to keep the train on the track for the long run. That was the point of it all, anyway. Not to prevent a derailment or train wreck. But to keep the train more safely and smoothly on the track.

Trail Log: Day 68

Coping Pitfalls
My Decision-Making

I WAS GETTING SO into this train-wreck thing that I drew a picture of it with a stick in the dirt this afternoon. Not that I wish that on me. But it resonated with me. I've forgotten why I got into the train in the first place. For a smooth ride, not to avoid a wreck.

I closed my eyes and thought about what decisions I've made while in this canyon. Along the way. Sometimes, little things. Sometimes, bigger things. It was interesting. But unsettling. Not to beat myself up or anything like that. But I've come to know that *I've become reactive.* I've stopped living within me. And begun to live outside of me. I've let everything around me color the *choices* that I make for me each day. In the spirit of keeping control, I've lost all control. Even the little that I actually have. Here goes...

I've made decisions on my own. Not that I have anyone traveling with me. But I do have trail guides and maps. Sometimes, I refuse to even look at them. I decide to do it on my own. On other days, I don't do any thinking on my own. I let the guide maps dictate everything to me. I abdicate it all. To a piece of paper or a compass. My brain checks out.

Then, on other days, I refuse to make any decisions at all. I get paralyzed. Stuck. Frozen. So I go nowhere. Just stand there. Standing in place. Hanging around. Nowhere, actually. Or I do the opposite, and make decisions really, really quickly. Without any thought or information. Just do it. Do it now. Do it fast. Time's a wasting. So am I when I do that.

When I suffer, my *decision-making* suffers. I need to be far more curious and purposeful. My decisions need to emanate from me. Within me. Mindfully. More consistently. If I would do that more, my decisions would be better. Safer. More considered. Wiser. And benefit me in the end. And isn't that what good, sound decisions are meant to be?

Good for me. Coming from me. On the basis of knowing that they're already in me.

Trail Log: Day 69

Coping Pitfalls

Mangled Bicycle Wheel

ON YESTERDAY'S WALK, I happened to see a bike wheel tossed over at the edge of a rock clearing. I was curious about it, as I don't see many signs of civilized life here. The wheel was rusted, which was no surprise. The elements out here aren't kind to metal, rubber, aluminum, or anything really for that matter. Nothing lasts in this place. When I reached the wheel, I saw that it was also all mangled up. Distorted and bent to create this somehow almost oblong shape for the wheel and tire. Obviously, the rider had hit a bump on the trail and had lost control. And the tire's original shape 'lost' in that encounter.

Trying to cope with my suffering is a lot like the now-distorted wheel. When things were going famously, it seemed easy to keep a *balance of things in my life*. I had time for my health, my Spirituality, my relationships, my work, my leisure, my school, and my continuous development as a person and a professional. Now, the wheel wasn't exactly circular. Some things had somewhat greater or lesser priority. For example, I paid attention to my diet and nutrition. I exercised regularly. Maybe I needed more sleep each night. But I got it broadly balanced. On the Spiritual side, I made time for God and church. On the relationships side, I had time for family, friends, and some groups. I was working, going to school, and even had time for some fun hobbies on the weekend. All the elements were in relatively good balance more or less, I'd say.

But then I got sick. Then I lost my best friend. Then I lost my job. Then I seemed to lose my life, really. And the balance between the elements went completely out of sync. I spent all of my waking energy on my health. Everything else hit the skids. I let the rest of my life take a 'bike hike'. And I now realize that this wasn't coping well.

I need to maintain a better sense of balance in me. Like a functional, working bicycle wheel that actually holds me up.

Trail Log: Day 70

The Intersection of Coping

Today, I came upon a major fork in the road on this crazy canyon trail. The trail guide wasn't particularly clear. I needed to make a decision on the right way to go. After freaking out about it for a few minutes, I took a deep breath. I remembered my thoughts on decision-making. I decided against being the engineer on the 'train-wreck express'.

I took some bearings with my compass, looked at the map, looked around for markers. Took my time. And it all worked out. I'm on the right track now. Thankfully. Good one. I had hit an intersection and I came through it safely.

My suffering is like that sometimes. When some new or different crisis hits me, it's like I'm speeding up as I approach the intersection. So I'll make it through before the light changes. But the light changes. In the split second I have, I slam on the breaks. *Red Light.* Sudden stop. My suffering and loss can be like the sudden red light. I can't catch my breath. I'm numb. I'm in shock. I can't make any sense of things in the moment. I can't make decisions. Stuck. . .

Then sometimes, I'm coming to the intersection and hit an *Amber Light.* That's even worse than the red light sometimes. In my suffering, the amber light is like this ambivalent mix of hope, realism, and despair. Back and forth between them. In some no-man's land. Do I proceed through the intersection or do I stop? Nothing is clear. It's all jumbled up. . .

Sometimes, it's a *Green Light*, though. A sign that I can proceed. I can make some decisions. I can try to understand my losses. I can begin to make some sense of them. Some meaning. I can take a few steps forward today, however tentatively.

Now, I've heard it said that suffering and loss happen in a sequence. First this. Then that. Forget about that. There's nothing neat or linear about it. Instead, it's a thousand forks in the road. Lots of intersections. Lots of traffic lights. Flexible, fluid coping as I drive.

Trail Log: Day 71

Coping—Another Way
Information

WHEN I HIT THOSE fluid and crazy intersections of coping with my pain, I need better tools. I couldn't think straight while I walked today. So I took a seat on a large rock and rested for a few. And since there's no one out here in this canyon to talk with, I needed to look within myself. In the end, I have the answers inside of me anyway. If only I take the time to look there. I asked myself how others have coped with their losses and sorrows better than me. What were they doing that I'm not? Or, what have I done myself to cope more effectively with bad stuff in the past? When I was doing it better than usual. Got it right.

I realized that one tool for coping is *Information*. Facts. Data. But not just information. An *understanding of it*. When others have helped me cope, they've been able to help me get the right information. They've checked for my own understanding of things. They've asked me questions to sense what I know. How much I'm able to take in at the moment.

They've been willing to repeat things to me. Even when they're getting tired of doing so. Or thinking that I'm a dunce. Because they know that I'm not. I'm simply numb and confused. People who help me cope have facilitated my asking questions. Reassured me that there are no dumb ones. They're all good. They've advocated for me. Helped me to find my voice with others as I've asked the questions. Sometimes asked them for me when I've lost my voice. Or my way.

And they've stood up for using plain language. They've helped me wade through the jargon of language that no one understands. They say, "Please translate that for us. Into something we can actually grasp."

And the 'experts' don't say, "I don't know," when I ask a question. If they don't know, they tell me what they *do* know. Then they get the answers that I need to cope in the midst of it.

When I've been able to help others cope, I've done exactly the same thing for them.

Trail Log: Day 72

Coping—Another Way
Linkages

As I was having a quick breakfast before starting out again today, I thought about this canyon trail system. It's complicated. One trail links into another. Kind of. Actually, it's more like a maze. Sometimes, I feel like a rat running in it, to be sure. The trails have color codes or blazes. But they wear off the rocks or trees sometimes. One trail blends into another. And, Wham, you're lost. Again. In the maze. Like a rat. But bigger.

When I suffer, I feel like everything that I need is too complicated. I'm already hurting and tired. And the *system that surrounds my pain* doesn't make it one bit easier on me.

When people have helped me cope in the past, they've come alongside me in the maze. They've helped me to *navigate* it all. Like a compass doubling as a friend. They take my hand and guide me through it. All of it. They help me to make sense of the mindboggling network of my doctors, nurses, counselors, administrators, insurance agencies, collection agencies. It's like they've been my agent, actually. For all of the agencies. And everyone else.

They've not only helped me navigate through it all. They've also helped to close the loops in the midst of it all. They've helped me to stay connected in the system. To ensure my follow-up with the right people. Kept people to their promises. Kept things honest, upright, and afloat. Especially when I'm sinking. Fast.

Through it all, though, they've helped me most in this way: Sometimes I don't know what I don't know. That's the most dangerous part. It's the linkages that I don't even know that I have to make. Or the ones that I've missed. Friends have helped me to know what I don't know, but really need to know. Now I know. It's good to know that. I thank them for that. They've connected the dots and kept them connected. They've closed the gaps. They've stopped the leaks.

And when I've been able to help others cope, I've done exactly the same thing for them.

Trail Log: Day 73

Coping—Another Way

Keeping Me in Touch

WHEN YOU WALK IN this canyon, you can get lost. Not lost in the sense of losing your way on the trail. I've done that enough for a lifetime. I mean something different here, though.

I can get lost in the enormity of this place. Like lost in space. It's easy to lose a sense of 'me' in the midst of this trek sometimes. When I suffer, it feels a lot like that. I get lost. I lose touch with the most important part of the equation: Me. And when this happens, I need someone to help me to cope with it.

Those who've helped me in the past come close and listen. Really listen to me. They don't open up by telling me stuff. . . shoving lots of stuff into my now-dazed brain. No. They ask me what I understand is going on. They want to know what I think I know so far. It's not rocket science, really. Questions like "What happened, what did you see, what did you experience, what did you hear, and what was it like for you?" They want to *understand me before they tell me*. That's a radical concept, now isn't it? Way out there.

Not only this, but people who help me cope ask me about how I'm holding up under the weight of it all. Today. This moment. Not like some general "How's it going, buddy?" question. Because today is not yesterday. Now is not earlier today. Now is 'now'. And now my life has just crashed and burned. Now is the only thing that's on my mind. Now.

Even more, friends who help me cope ask me about my feelings. They acknowledge those feelings reverently. They feed them back to me, so that these feelings are affirmed. Real friends don't say dumb stuff like, "Don't worry. This will all work out. You'll get through it. Be strong, buddy." Today, it doesn't feel like it's all going to work out. Simply *be* with my feelings and coping.

When I've been able to help others cope, I've done exactly the same thing for them.

Trail Log: Day 74

Coping—Another Way

Keep it Simple

When I have 'down' days on the trail, I sometimes overthink things. I play out these weird fantasies about what might happen if. . .? When? How? I start to wind myself up with all the stuff that *might* happen down the road. Far down the road, to be more exact. And the more I fret about it, the more anxious I get. I start weaving this spectacular nuclear dumpster fire story in my mind. Probably going to rage out of control. Then *I'm* out of control. I've actually gone nuclear over the whole thing. On myself. Unnecessarily so. My coping can be a lot like that sometimes. It's like some self-fulfilling prophesy that I've created. What a shock when it later actually turns out exactly that way. . . no duh.

Friends or family who've helped me cope have helped me to stop this stuff. Not helpful. They've helped me to *Keep it Simple. Chunk it down.* By a lot. Down to bite size pieces. And they've stayed off their soapboxes. They've resisted the temptation to pontificate. They've shut down their prophesying for the day. No snappy, cheap talk about some day. Because right now is the only thing I control. This moment.

What matters most in the rush of suffering is simplicity. Like helping me with the basics. Like food. Water. Getting me to the bathroom in a strange place. Bringing me tissues when I need to cry. A lot. Helping me to get where I need to go next. Not tomorrow. But now. Today, already. They help me to decide the little things. Not the big picture stuff. I'll do that later.

They help to keep me company. Get friends or family to stay with me. Keep me from falling off the cliff. Because they've helped me to focus on the here and now. Nothing more. Frankly, I'm overwhelmed and shouldn't overthink anything at the moment. It's simply not useful. So in the end, I need someone to center me where I need to be. Here.

When I've been able to help others cope, I've done exactly the same thing for them.

Trail Log: Day 75

Coping—Another Way

Find a Friend

To be honest, this coping thing has been hard to digest. I've had some really good ideas over the past few days. I've reflected on my own coping tools when I've faced prior illnesses and my many crises. I've explored what others have done to help me to cope more effectively. And I've also come to understand that I've done the very same things for others along the way.

I wonder this, though: Maybe the coping tool that I need most is not a tool or a discipline or a specific practice at all. Maybe it's not even a buddy or a friend or a family member who's best helped me to cope. No. Think more expansively. What if *God is the Greatest Coping Master* in my life and in the lives of others?

Now, you might ask where God got God's own coping experience, anyway. For God's had it all covered from the get-go. Had the big picture and the plan from the jump. In any event, why would God need to cope, anyway? Huh. . . Well, for one, God has to deal with us. Our shenanigans. Our U Turns come seemingly out of nowhere. We humans keep God on God's toes. All day and all night. Things are never slow on this front for God. Full plate.

In his famous Beatitudes in the Book of Matthew, Jesus blessed the poor in spirit, the mourning, the meek, those who hunger for righteousness and mercy, the pure in heart, the peacemakers, the persecuted, and the reviled. Perhaps Christ was trying to encourage them to persevere and strive to cope as best they could in the midst of it.

But maybe, just maybe, Christ may have been saying this: Human life is not easy. It's full of messiness and randomness and losses and sickness and death. But those of you who face these trials are special in God's eyes. God will help you to cope with them or to overcome them. And better yet, you are most special in God's eyes precisely *because* you suffer with courage and faith. Then Christ says, "So jump on board my back. The Coping Express."

Final Thoughts for This Leg

THANK YOU, GOD, FOR yet another leg completed. I can't imagine where I'd be now without your presence and guidance. Without your inspiration and energy. Without your constant companionship. Coping with the compounding misery of this canyon is my biggest challenge. It's been an especially tough road.

I've come to understand on this leg that my coping skills haven't been all that great, after all. In reality, much of how I cope isn't healthy in the least. It's maladaptive. It feels like it works. But it's a Band-Aid on a major bleed. I've been trying to keep the trains running throughout these past months and years. As if my forward motion might magically heal my wounds. As if I might wear out my maladies. As if they might get tired and take off. Unfortunately, they do not. They're here. My decision-making has been rocky. Because my goal was to keep things going. In the same direction. Wrong direction, I'm afraid. And in the process of keeping on keeping on, I've become unbalanced. All my energy and focus is trained on my pain.

With your help, Lord, I need to take a step back. I need to rethink my coping skills. Build new muscles. Stretch them out a bit. Please help me to slow down. To get the facts. Think things through. Find a friend to talk about them with. A friend to help me stay better connected to the spinning plates around me. Keep me plugged into all the right sockets on the wall of my suffering. And, in so doing, I need to chuck things down. Focus on the most important thing today. For today. Not for next month or next year. But to think on and pray on the 'one big thing' today. Even if it's a little thing. Sometimes less is something more. I need to remember that more. And more.

And I need your help in all of this, God. More. I can't do it on my own. I shouldn't have to. And I needn't do so. If only I stay plugged into you more, God. Plugged in. Circuits running. Lights on. Amen.

Canyon Trail Leg Eight:
The Path of Healing and Transformation

"O sing to the Lord a new song; sing to the Lord, all the earth. Sing to the Lord, bless his name; tell of his salvation from day to day. Declare his glory among the nations, his marvelous works among all the peoples. For great is the Lord, and greatly to be praised; he is to be revered above all gods."

PSALM 96: 1–4

Leg Eight Canyon Trail Preview

THANK YOU, GOD, FOR sustaining me on the last leg. As I await the start of the next leg of the trail, I can't help but let my mind wander a bit. If I close my eyes, I can see a vision. I'm picturing this place of paradise. Bright and sunny with clean, crisp air. That I can breathe in without struggling to catch my breath. The trails are wide and flat. Easily traversable. My backpack is always full. I have lots of water to drink. Always fresh and cool. I always have the right gear. I'm just warm enough. Never hot. Never cold. And lots of spots to rest. In the shade. Where I can look out and around me. Expansive, gorgeous views. Of your amazing creation. While I gaze into this beauty, lots of fellow travelers stop to chat. We talk about our trips. The weather. Our friends and family back home. Our future plans. Our past glories. The joys of now. The forecast for tomorrow is more of the same. And for the next day after that. And the next week. Sunny skies.

But then I open my eyes. It's not nearly as sunny as that. I'm too busy getting out of here to look up very often. No time to stop and gaze. I need to get to the next stopping point and make camp for the night. Please, God, help keep me provisioned. With enough to get me through it all. But even more, help me to find something special and memorable in this place of desolation and loneliness. Help *this place* to make some difference in me. For having made the trek. Help the sun to come out every so often. And be the voice of a friend who stops and sits with me. And shares with me. A new and better story about me. Thanks, in advance, Lord.

Trail Log: Day 76

Creating a New Story

I AM BECOMING MORE keenly aware of my progress of late. As I begin this new leg of my journey, I am now far closer to the canyon's end than to the beginning. I'm learning about myself and my suffering along the way each day. I'll have many stories to tell others when I emerge from this place. And the stories will be sacred ones for sure. I have been formed through this journey of suffering to some extent, but it can't define me. It won't define me... unless I let it. I'll learn from it, but I will *not* be anchored to it. I'll write a new sacred story about me. I am the author of the story. God inspires. I write.

Part of my new story is my consciousness coming of age. In the solitude of this canyon, I've learned that I need to make me more conscious of myself. More attuned. In touch. I've lived too much of my life unconsciously. I've reacted to things. To others. To stuff. To slights. To hurts. To my losses. To the unfairness that's accompanied me of late.

The worst part of it all is this: I responded and reacted unconsciously. When I'm angry and not curious about it, I simply act out. Often irrationally. If I were to look back on it years from now, I'd scratch my head. What was that all about? What the heck. Why in the world? It's like my soul is on autopilot. Just beneath the surface. Reacting unconsciously to my suffering in ways that don't help me one bit. Not even a little.

I lash out, shut out, push out, deflect away, deny it all, and withdraw from it all. Then repeat it all. Again and again. Like an assembly line of unconscious self-annihilation.

The source of my pain lies *within* me. And so does the healing. And the transformation. I need to move what's at the back of my mind to the front of my mind. And to my heart. Be open, honest, and curious about it. Bring it fully into my presence. Work with it.

Sure, it's tough and painful. But it's what I don't know and feel that's killing me.

Trail Log: Day 77

Movement Forward

BRINGING THINGS INTO MY consciousness is like writing my story in the dirt of this canyon. I take a stick or a stone and sketch in the sandy soil. I map it all out with lines and circles and figures and the like. What a grand picture on the path! And then I walk away. I can't take a picture of it. I didn't bring a camera with me in this place. So, it's simply left to sit. But it doesn't really. The rains come. The winds howl. The boots of other feet squash it. It's like it was frozen in time until it wasn't. It was wiped away.

My healing is a lot like that, I think. The picture story of me in the dirt is nothing more than that. Unless I do something with it. I need to dream big, of course. Dream about recovery. About new starts. New possibilities. New probabilities. New friends. New. But I need to do so much more. I need a more detailed storyboard of my life. A sacred story of where I'm now going. A storyboard not locked in the dirt like some lifeless portrait. No. I need to *lift* the picture from the sandy soil and make it live. Alive in 3-D.

That takes setting goals and planning for success. It takes courage. The courage to put my toes in the water and try it out. My toes may tingle with cold or burn with heat at the water's touch. Or I might fall into the water headfirst. Or jump like a belly flop or a cannon ball. I need to push myself to try it out, though. Sometimes I need others to give me a loving nudge. I may have to close my eyes or hold my nose or cover my mouth. I may have to negotiate this jumping-in thing with smaller incremental steps. But I need to get in the pool.

I must come to terms with this notion: I have suffered. I have lost. I have experienced pain. And I am now changed because of it. There is no going back. There is no baseline in my rearview mirror. There is only here. And now. This moment in time. I need a plan of action and some actions to work the plan. I need to take the first step.

Trail Log: Day 78

Reflection on my Actions

So, let's pretend that I'm somehow able to take this sketch of my new life off the ground. Literally lift it out of the dirt. Put it on some transformational canvas that I can somehow carry with me on the trail. I dream big and love the details. I'm a planner and a doer. So this canvas is going to be a heavy, bulky one. I need a bigger backpack to carry it.

But unless it changes along the way, I've done nothing more than simply carry it along. I've written a tome which now rests somewhere in my pack. Not a tome, actually. A tomb. Like some homage to my story in some museum. Or mausoleum. Or grave. The only way that I change and grow through this trek is to change and grow *as I go*.

Having my new storyboard, my vision, my goals, and my plan is just great, as it were. But I need to take some breaks along the way. Just like when I'm hiking this canyon. I need to take a breather. To reflect on the plan en route. Ask lots of questions about it. Maybe it was great on the canvas, but no so great in action. Maybe it was a great plan, but stuff came up. And I got blown off course for a while. Maybe it was working just fine, but it was wearing me out. It was fine. I wasn't. I need to be fine, too, sister.

I need to stay curious, reflect on my progress, and make corrections along the way. Course corrections. Get back on track. Set a slightly new path. Think about how I can maintain the progress that I've actually made thus far. Celebrate my successes. Take a breath. Get some sleep. Write down my thoughts before I go to sleep. Wake up and write some more. Keep a log. Log my place. Set my bearings. Then set some new ones.

Based on how it's gone. What I've learned. How it's worked. What might work better. What I need to do more of. What I need to say 'no more' to. When I can simply say 'no'. When I embark on changing myself, the changes themselves change too. That's OK.

Trail Log: Day 79

Incorporation without Refreezing

So, now I have this plan for changing me. I'm creating a new story about myself. Without leaving myself behind... in the dirt. And the changes are changing along the way as I reflect and course-correct. That's correct. No corrections necessary to that thought.

But here's my problem with this whole thing: It's really, really hard to resist my need to refreeze. This unfreezing thing is hard work. Change is tough stuff. Sometimes brutal.

Isn't the point of the whole thing to transform me, and then refreeze in my new 'normal'? My new, transformed self. Like a shiny new car on the sales lot. All polished and buffed up. It's even got the new car smell. The perfectly clean floor mats. The unscratched dashboard. The perfect sightlines on the mirrors. Who wants to mess with that anyway? I'm going to drive this beauty home and put it in the garage. Lock the door and never use it again. So the newness thing is cast in stone forever. Like a piece of jewelry in a case.

It all sounds so good. Get to my new baseline. My new normal. Then keep it set. I'm set. But the new thing, the new me, is like a new car. It needs to be driven. If I leave it as is, the metal will rot. Dust will settle. The fuel line will corrode. The spark plugs will get stale. And the car won't start when I need it to someday. It will have died the death of neglect. It may still look nice, but it won't run nice. In fact, it won't run at all in the end.

So, as nice as this refreezing thing sounds, I can't ever do that. I need to incorporate my changes in me. The new me. Then keep on keeping on. Keep the water flowing beneath the surface so the water can't freeze. Or refreeze. It may glaze over from time to time, but it can't ever refreeze. Frozen is good for ice-skating and popsicles. That's about it.

It's not good for planes or boats or cars or bicycles. Or people. It's bad for everything that moves. Bad for me. Even when it feels good or sounds good. I'm not a popsicle.

Trail Log: Day 80

Becoming More 'Whole'

As I was walking the trail yesterday, I began to think about what will happen when I actually walk out of the canyon. I'm clear about my goals. I'm taking actions to move me in that direction. I'm reflecting and course-correcting along the way, I suppose. But it may not mean much in the end if I'm not 'whole' in the process. Transforming me starts from within, not from without. It's a 'do it yourself' kind of a project.

So... I'm picturing me as a big pie with four large slices, each of equal size. The *first slice* of me is *my oneness with me*. I need to get in touch with things like my sense of hope, my fears and anxiety, my losses, my sense of my body image (how do I think I look to others and why), my areas of guilt and shame, my coping, and my identity. But most of all, I need to check my 'agency': How much of my suffering am I owning? Have I become a victim?

The *second slice* of me is my *oneness with others*. How healthy are my relationships? Where is my loving support coming from and why? If from nowhere, why not? How isolated and lonely do I feel and why? And what do I need to do about it to better connect with others?

The *third slice* of me is my *oneness with the environment* around me. I need to recognize that, for most in this world, the pie is not cut equally. The 'least' live far less well than others. Our planet is suffering and neglected, too. I can't change everything, but I need to open my eyes more to things that aren't right. Then keep my eyes open and start doing something about it.

The *last slice* of me is my *oneness with transcendence*. Where am I on my search for greater and more transcendent meaning, purpose, and healthier values? How do I view God? Do I feel punished or abandoned? What are my concepts of death, dying, and eternity? Why?

With all this said, I need all four slices of the 'me' pie to be whole. And healthy. So... I have some baking to do.

Trail Log: Day 81

Becoming 'Healthier'

I WOKE UP THIS morning under a large ledge. It was raining pretty hard. The trail was covered in mud. It was cold and I could feel a chill in my bones. But I rustled about and began to get up. I needed to push on today, no matter what. Had to keep making progress.

But then I thought about it a little more. What's gained with one day traveled if I get sick and lose three more days in even greater misery? Whose clock is timing me, anyway? So, I crawled back under my sleeping bag and stayed warm. And dry. And snug. Nice.

As I lay there, I thought about how hard I've pushed myself my whole life. I'm always saying, "Got to power through it all. The world keeps on going. So do I. If not me, who else? Keep pushing on." And I've paid a price for that. It's made my suffering worse. It may have even caused some of it. If I'm ever going to transform me, I need to change the way I think about me.

When I get out of this canyon of suffering, I need to give myself a break. I need more sleep each day. I need to eat better, like everything really depends on it. Because it does. I need to pay attention to my stress levels. Then do something about them. And I need to take time for exercise. The first thing each day. If I fall back into doing nothing, everything I've gained on this long hike out will be for naught. That makes me naughty. Not in a good kind of way.

And I need to pay attention to exercising my brain. That's a part of me, too. I need to keep stretching my mind. I need to build new skills. Not just this, but I need to broaden my interests in life. Take some of those big eggs out of the single basket. Spread them around. Create new baskets. Lay some new eggs. Good eggs.

Lastly, I need to get out more. Join some clubs. Join friends. Join the gym. Join something somewhere somehow that'll get me out of my own head.

So, in the end, I need to keep stretching me. I'm elastic after all. I stretch more than I think I do.

Trail Log: Day 82

Becoming More Creative

THE DAY OFF YESTERDAY did me a world of good. I feel more rested. Today is a much nicer and dryer day. The ground is still a bit muddy, but I can manage that OK. When I made my decision to 'not proceed' yesterday, I sat under the ledge while the rain fell. I'd really never watched the rain before. I'd seen it simply as a stopper or blocker. But I closely watched it yesterday. I got intrigued by the channels that the rain dug in the dirt. As the hours wore on, the lines of water went in new directions. New ways. New shoots. In ways unrelated to those before, but fascinating, actually. In order to go with the flow, the ground had to let go of its former certainties— its form and placement. It had to let go.

So do I, actually. Even in my suffering. Because I have to get more creative about healing. I've let my need for sameness and comfort get in the way. So have the judgment and criticisms of me by others. Because I let them. So have my fear and pessimism. Because I let them. Frankly, so have my self-imposed limitations and boundaries. Because I let them.

In order to transform and heal me, I need to think *outside the box*. I need to look at my problems not just as symptoms any longer. What's really going on underneath them? I have to quit putting Band-Aids on hemorrhages. I need to start asking different questions about my suffering. I have to start talking to different people. I need to look at it from different perspectives. I need to step out of my emotions sometimes to look at it more objectively. Frankly, I need to become more curious about it overall.

I keep doing the same stuff over and over and over again. Then I'm surprised that I always get the same results. Nothing changes. Nothing ever will. Until I actually think in new ways. Act in new ways. 'Be' in new ways. Until I get out of my comfy, safe, but suffering head and box for a while. Then create a new one. But never 'live' in one.

Trail Log: Day 83

Becoming More Forgiving

As I continued thinking about this whole 'get out of my box' thing, I became angry. With each step I took, I felt this churning in my stomach. I felt stress and tension in my chest. I got fixated on all the wrongs that were done to me. By a lot of people along the way. By my family, my co-workers, and my so-called friends. Bad stuff. I never seemed to know what the 'enemy' was up to. I never saw it coming from people whom I trusted. And I got busted. I'm still getting busted. I'm in this canyon, after all.

I started thinking about how I've tried to forgive others in the past. But it wasn't really forgiveness. I cut them a break. I gave them leniency. I tried to forget about it. I justified it. And I asked God to punish these so-and-sos for their evil. "Blast them, God!" Maybe this wasn't forgiveness after all. I hadn't let it go. I pushed it away. I buried it. I denied it. I decided that the bad guys didn't deserve me. I decided to rise above it. I devalued the apologies of others. They're not sincere, anyway.

I became a victim. And it became a prison. A wall which cut me off from others, from myself, and the world. It became a cancer that's now metastasizing into my bones. Spreading. Shutting me down. And in the end, I was the only one suffering. This means that I suffered twice. Once from the hurt of others. And once by the hurt I inflicted on myself. Double jeopardy. I lose. Twice.

The only way I can heal is to forgive. Forgive the past. Forgive others. Forgive myself. Forgive the universe. Forgive with healthier boundaries. But forgive and move on. Forgiving is in my own hands, actually. Not anyone else's. I need to decide. Then work at it every day. Name it. Tell the other. Write a letter. Meditate on it. Then actually move on with things. Freely. When I do so, I take back my power. The only real power that I really have in the end. The power to start anew. The power to think anew. The power to be something new.

Trail Log: Day 84

Becoming More Integral

ONE OF THE BIGGEST things I need to forgive is 'me'. Actually, I'm not a thing. But sometimes I feel like it. Especially when I'm hurting and sad. Or angry and mad.

As I walk this trail out, I've thought about the trail itself. The trail is a path. It's a way from the beginning to the end. Grounded in something bigger than the path itself. Aligned with the best way out of the canyon. While the path may 'zig' and 'zag', the turns are always the turns. The trail doesn't reinvent itself each day. It's a trail. It's consistent and it reminds me daily that there *is* an end to this canyon. A way to the truth. The truth of a new, healthier, transformed me.

The beauty of the trail is its integrity. I can count on it. And even though the scenery changes each moment, the trail is steady. Even though I face obstacles, the trail is steady. The trail is here today. It'll be here tomorrow. *I* need to have more integrity, too, actually. In order to heal. I need to become more like the trail.

I've let my short term goals get in the way. I've lost the big picture. Lost the trail. I've let poor role models get me off the trail. I've let my losses steer me askew. I've let unhealthy boundaries in relationships push me asunder. I've let my lack of daily discipline bog me down.

While I need to stretch and grow and change, I also have to chart a course. A trail map of sorts. I need to have a clearer vision about where I want to go. Who I really am and who I want to be in my life. I need to get clear on the things that move me onward toward this vision. And things that hinder my progress each day. If I get clearer about this and am willing to be honest and authentic about it, I can live with more integrity.

It's not easy to have integrity, to be fair. It's a bit like swimming upstream sometimes. But if I'm more purposeful about it, I can achieve the greatest prize of all. I can keep my word to others. I can keep my word to myself. I can live more integrally. Honest to goodness.

Trail Log: Day 85

Becoming More Generous

I WAS RIFLING THROUGH my pack today and realized that my rations are running short. I've been trying to 'live off the land' as much as possible. And stay on track each day. I only have so much food left. And there are no fast food joints on the trail. No express food marts. No grocery stores. No sit-down diners. No gourmet food trucks. I'm on my own. And, to be honest, I worry about it. I can't eat dirt. Low nutrition stuff. Tastes bad.

But maybe I worry too much. When I fixate on having enough of something, I hoard it. I get less hopeful. I get more hoard-full. And all I worry about is being full... of it. Maybe I worry too much about a lot of things, actually. Not just my food. Maybe I've spent way too much of my life hoarding everything. Gathering, collecting, protecting.

Maybe I've not given freely of my abundance to others. Maybe I've not shared enough. Maybe I've not shared kindness, stuff, time, energy, concern, empathy, and me. I've gone above and beyond for me and my own worries. I've gone below and beneath on the generosity front, I guess. I've made life a zero-sum game. I've seen the world as some finite prize that I need to claim. Need to get my share of, doggone it. Mine. My piece. Like it was some ruby or sapphire or diamond. That I didn't really need after all. Nope.

In order to heal and transform, though, I need to be more altruistic. I need to give with no expectation of getting anything back. I need to focus more on others and less on myself. I need to trust God, others, and the universe that things will work out. I need to be more optimistic and hopeful. I need to live more simply. Spend less. Give more. I need to open my eyes more and look around. Find opportunities to share more. Find something bigger than me. Something which transcends me. That can make this world a better place. Then get after it. Get It Done. Small steps. Taken generously. That's hopeful and healing.

Trail Log: Day 86

Becoming More God-Filled

THIS LEG OF THE trail has been darn near exhilarating. I've learned so much. About myself and the path ahead. I feel, for the first time, as if I'm onto something special. I can see a way forward through it all. And out of this canyon. Of my suffering and pain. I think I've done it. Congrats to me!!! Party time, everyone. . . Oh yeah, and it's only me. "Party of one. The best table in the house, please. In the corner, please. Away from everyone else, please. Where I can have some peace and quiet, please. By myself. To eat alone."

But what kind of a party is that, anyway? For if the new me is just 'me', who else is going to see me? Who am I going to share with? And even worse than that, I wouldn't be 'me' in the first place without the One who created me. In the first place. I wouldn't be breathing and smiling and crying and laughing and even living if it were up to me. I'm simply not capable of creating me. Of carrying me. Of sustaining me. Of giving breath to me. Of giving light to me. Life to me.

I may be 'me' and I may be new. But I'm really nothing without God. I'd never have changed without God. I'd never have made it. I'd never have kept keeping on. I'd never have survived it, even. Without God. For God is the author of my changes. Of my walk out of this canyon. I provide the hands and the feet and the sweat-equity for sure. But God gives me the sweat to cool down my forehead during the heat of the day. I walk the path of healing for sure. But God provides the ground on which I walk. I try to stay as steady as possible. But God picks me up when I fall. I try to keep going when I'm just about ready to give up for sure. But God never gives up on me.

So I need God. Simply arriving or 'becoming' is nothing special. Nor is being 'me' without God's being 'in me' in the first place. For I'm a human being after all. All of me. And God has it all covered. All of it. All of me. Because God is all in all. Always.

Final Thoughts for This Leg

I AM GRATEFUL FOR your presence, Lord. For your filling me with your grace and your hope. And your promise. Something I can hold firmly to. Even when I can't hang on anymore. Thank you for holding a vision of 'healing' before me. Within my reach. Thank you for being the author of my own sacred story. It gives me strength to know that I don't need to write it all myself. I need to keep believing and dreaming. Big.

But I need to do far more than that. Dreams are simply dreams if I simply sit on them. I need to cultivate them. Plan for them. Help to make them happen. Help to make me happen along the way, too. Because none of it will happen without me. And my involvement. At the same time, though, I can't be a bull in the china shop. I need to periodically stop and reflect on my progress. My progress in healing and transformation. Then course-correct along the way. And I need to resist the biggest temptation of all: To arrive, then refreeze there. In truth, I can never allow myself to refreeze. Never again. No more frozen.

Lord, help me to heal by being more 'whole' as a person. By becoming healthier in my thoughts, my words, and my actions each day. Unleash my innate creative ability to think outside the box in my healing journey. Help me to forgive myself and others when I hit snags along the way. Guide me to be truer to myself and my values, even when I'm tempted to morph into something else in order to simply survive. Please give me a heart of generosity. For I have something to give others. I can give of myself, my time, my learned wisdom, my experiences, and my story. I can give out of my weakness and my wounded heart. The wounds that I wear make me more authentic to others. Because they say that I'm just like others. Wounded. Hurting. I need not even say a word. They know. God knows. Our wounds heal each other. Generously. Amen.

Canyon Trail Leg Nine:
When We Don't 'Heal'

"For it was you who formed my inward parts; you knit me together in my mother's womb. I praise you, for I am fearfully and wonderfully made. Wonderful are your works; that I know very well. My frame is not hidden from you, when I was being made in secret, intricately woven in the depths of the earth."

PSALM 139: 13–15

Leg Nine Canyon Trail Preview

ACCORDING TO THE TRAIL guide map, I'm about to hit a very steep grade ahead, Lord. It's all up-hill from here. You'd think they'd put the heavy incline stuff in the beginning of this trail. When I'm fresher with more energy to spare. Not toward the end. When I'm out of all energy. When my tank is empty. So what gives here? And to make this whole hill climb even more interesting, the map says that I can expect steady, heavy headwinds. Like a gale in my face. Right between my eyes. Blowing dirt and dust into my eyes. Like a fire hose of wind. Turned up to high. And no 'turn off' switch.

Given all this, I'm not sure I'm going to ever make it. I have nothing left, to be honest. And I now feel like giving up. Mailing it in. Sitting down and staying down. Waving the white flag. Of surrender. Come and get me. I'm done. Put a fork in me. Really done. Because it feels like I'll never leave this place after all. It's done me in. Who ever thought of putting the hardest part of the trail at the end, anyway, God? Did you have a hand in this? If so, you've now given me 'more' than I can handle.

But just when I most want to give up and give in, though, I need to keep going. Precisely now. And I'm asking you to help me find a way, God. To find a way precisely when there appears to be absolutely no way. When I most want to stop, please keep me on 'start'. When I most want to turn the lights out, please keep them 'on'. When I most want to lie down, please sit me up. When I most want to scream, put a song in my heart. When I most want to silence myself, put a prayer on my lips. When my heart wants to sputter and flutter and slow, keep it beating strongly, Lord. Please keep it beating. Thanks, in advance, God.

Trail Log: Day 87

Just Got the News

According to the trail guidebook, I thought I was actually nearing the end of this long walk out. I was starting to 'feel it'. Starting to actually 'smell it'. Starting to 'taste it'. But then 'it' happened yesterday. The trail just ahead was washed out from recent, heavy rains. The water levels were still quite high and didn't look to go down anytime soon. And there was no other way out. So I fell to my knees and cried. Not figuratively. No. Literally. With a volume of tears equal to the force of the raging stream which washed out the trail. Now I'm washed out.

My insides were fighting this terrible battle. Part of me wanted to flee. *Take flight*. Run away as fast as I could. It didn't matter where. Just run. Fast. And keep running and running and running and running. Anywhere but here. And when I couldn't run any longer, I would lay down under a rock. And curl up into the fetal position like a helpless baby. And rock myself to sleep. Using a stick as a pacifier.

Another part of me wanted to *fight*. To fight the utter unfairness of it all. The unjustness of it all. None of this was even remotely fair. I didn't deserve an ounce of this. I could wade across the stream. Hit the raging waters head-on. Take my chances. Probably die in so doing, but I simply didn't care anymore. Must get out of here now... or die trying.

The final part of me wanted to *freeze in place*. And to be honest, that's what happened. I simply froze. I couldn't think any longer. I couldn't feel any longer. I was a statue. Numb. Paralyzed. In place.

So, I stood and stared at the now-gone trail. My eyes must have looked blank. Totally blank. And I was now shooting blanks. I was out of bullets. My hopes of leaving this place... of healing as I knew it... were quite possibly over. It was like receiving a death sentence over the phone. "We're sorry to inform you that you're toast. Burned toast. Please call our customer service line with any questions."

Trail Log: Day 88

Taking Stock

So Now What?

I MUST HAVE STARED at the washed-out trail for nearly the entire day yesterday. Never took my eyes off of it. If I stared long enough, I hoped that the scenery might change. It didn't. Actually, it was worse than watching water boil over a nearly nonexistent flame. Or worse than watching paint dry on a humid day. At least the paint does something. The water eventually boils. I was doing nothing. And the scenery wasn't changing a bit. Not even a little.

As I woke up this morning to the same reality, I began to think about all the advice I've been given through the years. About suffering. In general. I've been told to ignore the pain. "If you forget about it, the whole thing will go away. It's all in your mind, anyway." I've been told to simply press on. "If you stay strong and push ahead, this will eventually pass." I've been told to be more stoic about my suffering. "Keep a stiff upper lip, buddy. Crying is weakness. Don't ever let them see your tears. You'll lose all respect." I've been told that I need to cry more. "If you don't cry about this, it means that you're not feeling it. Let it out. Cry up a river. You'll eventually cry it out."

In reality, though, all the sage advice is simply that. Some snappy lines of wisdom by some sage somewhere. Some wise-guy who doesn't get me. Because he never met me. He has no idea of what I'm going through. I'm not living this canyon in a book. No. I'm living it right here. In real-time. Right now. Right this minute. The trail is washed out.

So, I trashed the sage advice. I stepped back from the brink. And I turned the freezing into reflecting. About what's still possible for me. Even in the face of apparent calamity. I started taking stock. Of a lot of things. Because I might be stuck here in the end. To my end, actually. And, in the process, I began to think about all the accumulated stuff I have to shed. Not my external stuff. But my 'internal' stuff. To be free again. If I don't heal.

Trail Log: Day 89

Taking Stock

What's Still Possible?

AFTER SITTING AND REFLECTING some more for most of yesterday, I decided to press ahead on the trail. Actually, *backwards*, to be more accurate. I couldn't go forward. The trail was washed out. No telling how long the high waters would last. No safe way to cross what once was the trail. So I backtracked. In hopes of finding another way to return to the main trail out. Find a safer way to get back on track. I had hoped and prayed that I'd make it out 'my' way. This is no longer possible. In fact, I may never make it out. But I'm going to keep moving. In so doing, I've adopted a new mantra. 'What is still possible'?

This canyon has taken a toll on me. So has my incessant suffering. But it hasn't taken me yet. Maybe a lot of me. But not all of me. And I won't let the canyon or my suffering define me any longer. It's so easy to get drawn into the drama of this place and the total mess that I'm in. Fused to it like some welder drew a large bead on me. Stuck forever. Like a magnet on metal. But *I'm* not stuck. I still have my autonomy. No one place or thing or condition can define me unless I let it. It's easy to let it. But I can't. Or I'll get it.

I can no longer control the outcome of all of this. I may never get out. But I can try my best to find some meaning, purpose, values, and learning in the midst of it. I can try to use whatever time I have left to do the hard work of living. Yes, living is possible. Even in *this* place. I can start writing down my experiences in this canyon. What I've been going through. What I've learned. About this place. About myself. The 'about myself' part is the most important part.

Perhaps I need to rethink 'me', my purpose, and my meaning in the face of this adversity. Perhaps I need to reinvent myself in the face of my pain and loss. It's not easy. For I'm not some slinky or some play dough glob. But I can find something important in this space. Something new and special. Like me. Healed.

Trail Log: Day 90

Taking Stock

Of My Hope

As I backtracked my trek today, the trail looked different than it had going the other way. It was the same trail, of course. Obviously. I'm going backwards. But I'm seeing things from the opposite direction. The same, but different. And I'm wondering if I've gotten all caught up with my tunnel vision in this canyon? I've been looking only one way. Straight ahead. Stay on the trail. Keep a keen eye on what's just ahead. Stay on course. Blot out all the rest. The extraneous stuff. Get out of here. The only way out. Don't doddle. Don't waste time. Focus. Walk. Eat. Sleep. Walk. Focus. I made a fair amount of progress doing things that way. Until I hit the roadblock. The big one.

And now I need to rethink it all. Reinvent it all. It's darn daunting. And scary. Everything's changed. Except one thing. *Hope*. I don't have to surrender my autonomy. And I needn't give up my hope, either. If I do, I have nothing left. I'm officially a goner. Holding hope doesn't mean that the way out is certain. Because it's not. At all. Not anymore. But hope *does* mean that I stay open to the future. And its possibilities. And what they might mean for me.

I can also think about what's practical or doable right now. And how I'll handle the many setbacks and roadblocks now in front of me. Keep solving the problems as they come up. Then course-correct as necessary.

And I can come to terms with the alternative outcomes that I may now face here. I might find another way out. That would be good. Really good. Or someone might come along and rescue me. I'm good with that one, too. Or I may find a way to be at some peace here. Even if it's forever here. Not easy, but possible. Or, I may die in here. Not what I'm looking for. Not at all. Bad outcome, actually. But I can do even that with some dignity and self-respect. Yes, even if I die in here. I needn't let even *that* define me. Or my life. Because it doesn't.

Trail Log: Day 91

Taking Stock

Wishes and Fears

As I continued to walk today, I became increasingly anxious. I was now backtracking further and further. There appeared no other way to get back on the main trail out. No forks in the road. No clearings that might let me traverse the canyon sideways or something. I began to imagine a future in which I might not get out at all. In the end. That I might actually 'end' here. I sat down in the dirt under the shade of a rock wall.

I had 'hit the wall' literally and figuratively. I knew that accepting the 'reality' of this wasn't going to be linear. Sometimes I feel at peace with the possibility that I'll never get out. Sometimes it depresses me greatly. I feel like I'm getting sucked into a quicksand pit. Slowly but surely. And no one is there to extend a helping hand. And I sink. Sunk.

So I've started taking stock. Of my hopes and my fears. First, my hopes. To get out of this canyon alive. To see a future life in ways that somehow transcend my suffering. But I've been asking myself the second-level questions about my hopes. Like how this canyon trek might shape me in healthier ways some day? If I actually make it. And what difference can I make in the future as a result? How can I put what I've learned about me to better use? In a new, creative, reinvented me kind of way. Like artwork.

And now to my fears. What if I don't get out and die here? How do I feel about death? What might life after death look like? Why do I feel the ways that I do about it, anyway? Whose story am I buying on that score? And is the narrative a helpful one for me? Is my view of my death helping me to cope with and to face this possibility? Actually face it with hope and dignity. Not with distress and loathing and fear. How might I look at death in ways that make it more meaningful to me and to others? Further, how might I think about God in ways that allow God to help me in and through my death? If it's time.

Trail Log: Day 92

Taking Stock

Blessings and Losses

IF I EVER MAKE it out of here alive, I need to do an inventory. Not of my clothes and gear. Frankly, I don't have that much stuff. And everything I have is now worn out. No one would want it. Couldn't even give it away. When they find it, they'll trash it. Or bury it. Along with me. If I do make it, I'll get new stuff anyway. All new. So, I need to take an inventory. Not of my stuff. But of stuff, nonetheless. The stuff that's happened to me.

In the midst of my many canyon trials and tribulations, it's easy to look only at the bad stuff. I've certainly had more than my share of the bad stuff, for sure. But I need to stop the train for a second. Step back. And look at the blessings in my life. If 'me' is to end here, I need to remember that it wasn't always me 'here'. I've had many blessings along the way. I've had friends and family. I've had work and play. I've had gifts and abundance. I've had good and even great food along the way. I've toasted others at parties. I've been toasted by others. The champagne variety. Not the 'toast' that I seem to be now. I've had good deeds done for me. And I've done them for others. I've had joyful, wonderful times. I've seen amazing things and places. I've been graced with grace. Had second chances when I didn't deserve them. I've been forgiven. Even when I couldn't forgive others. I've been loved. When I didn't deserve it.

For sure, I've had lots of losses, as well. More than I can even remember. For life is also a series of losses. Small and big. One at a time. Sometimes in big bunches. Loss is a fact of life. It just is. And I need to take stock of them all. But I don't need to live in them. For life is not simply about what I can no longer do. About what is no longer. What can be no more.

No. It's about what life has brought my way, as well. The many, many blessings I've enjoyed along the way. Even here in this canyon. Even here. Believe it or not. Even here. In this canyon.

Trail Log: Day 93

Taking Stock
Of My Past

If I should die right here in this crazy canyon, I need to take stock. Of my life. I've long since decided to take time each day to write this daily trail log you'll be reading if someone finds me. Or at least finds my trail log. Writing the log has been cathartic. It's given me the chance to tell my story of this place. This place of suffering. And of hope. And of my learning. And my feelings. The good stuff and the bad stuff. All of it.

But I need to start another project. I should take some time to write about my history. To take stock of my life. For I've decided that I won't be known by my losses or pains or sorrows or even my death. And certainly not by this canyon trail. I've walked it and lived it, to be certain. But I've not become it. Not even remotely. Even though it is remote.

I need to tell the story of my *legacy*. To stop focusing so much on fretting the future. For, in truth, I can actually influence very little of it at this juncture. I certainly need to spend more time in the present. But part of that 'present' time for me is visiting the *past*. For my past is a present, a gift of sorts, which will outlive me. No holiday or birthday needed. I can spend some time celebrating. Now, I needn't wrap this gift in some fancy paper. Or put a bow on it. Or twirl lots of ribbon around the box. No. Just the opposite. I need to unwrap it a bit. Ideally, I'd share it with someone verbally. But that's simply not possible out here. Unless I talk to the ground squirrels. Tried it. Done that. No go.

But I *can* write it out on paper. And there's a story to tell underneath all the pain. I have done things. Accomplished things. Achieved some pretty cool things. Made a difference to others and to me along the way. I've grown and learned and stretched along the way. I've gained some wisdom after all, I guess. So, I have a lot to share in the end. Because I took time to take stock of my life. To look back proudly to my past. To me.

Trail Log: Day 94

Taking Stock

Of My Feelings About God

IF I'M COMPLETELY AND totally honest, here, I have to acknowledge some real anger. Sometimes some real rage. About this entire mess that I'm in. Yeah, in the canyon.

I have no one to talk to about it. For it's only me here at the moment. And nobody wants to hear my complaining anyway. Who has time for that these days? We all have our own problems. No need to pile mine onto the pile that belongs to someone else. Onto theirs.

And, some days, I'm not really 'feeling' God, either. The very fact that I'm admitting this is giving me some angina. Some heart palpitations. Some jitters. And some real guilt. For who am I to be angry with God? Anyway. Just little ole me looking up to the sky and cursing the 'Big Guy' out. Probably not in my own best interest in all likelihood.

So, I shut myself up about the whole God-doubt thing. The whole God-silence thing. Sometimes, I just quit thinking about God at all. Given that I can't be mad at God.

But, then I was thinking the other day. Why can't I be angry with God? Really miffed. Like, if I get mad, God will shrink away and hide? Or sit and sulk in the corner of Heaven. Or send ten lightning bolts my way. Special delivery. Same-day canyon service. No signature required. In fact, there'll be no one left to sign it. Spat. Zap. Zing. The former me has just been 'offed'. By God. Thanks for playing. Now be gone.

No. That's not the way it actually works. We *can* be angry with God. God's got big shoulders. God can listen to us. And weep with us. And stay with us through the night.

And it's this simple in the end: I can't be angry with someone I don't believe in. If there's no God, there's no transcendent one to share my feelings with. In the end, God is bigger and more powerful than my fears, my trepidations, my limitations, my times, my vision, my understanding. Even my hopes. God is listening. God is whispering. If only I listen.

Trail Log: Day 95

Taking Stock
Letting Go

IF I DON'T MAKE it out of this canyon alive, some people will say that I quit on myself. I surrendered. My losses and pain beat me in the end. I lost the big battle. To my end. And that might seem logical to many. For life is a battle. Of winners and losers. We either win. . . or we lose. Quite simple, actually. Tidy. Clean. Neat. Until you step back and look at it.

If they find me here and I'm no longer 'here', if you know what I mean, I didn't surrender. I didn't lack courage or persistence or the will to keep fighting the good fight. I didn't succumb to my fears or my anxieties or my worst instincts. I simply didn't make it out.

In the days and weeks ahead, I need to make the most of the time that I do have left. And that may mean, at some point, letting go. *Letting go is not giving up*. Not even close. If, at some point, I have to let go, it means that I've come to a peace. An inside peace that I've done all that I can. Peace which knows that I couldn't have done anything else. Peace which understands that, sometimes, nature simply takes its course.

Peace which knows the difference between prolonging life and allowing natural death. If it comes to that. Peace which 'gets' quality of life really, really well. Quality that makes my remaining days meaningful. As joyful as possible. Surrounded by the things that give me peace here. Letting go means that I've come to terms with the inevitable. Then stop trying to fight it. And begin to live within it. Preserve my strength when fighting is no longer the best option. Get and keep comfortable. Manage my pain. Finish the unfinished stuff in my life. Say my goodbyes to everyone. Even if I can't say these in person.

Letting go isn't fear or weakness or giving up. Letting go is hard and courageous. I hope that I don't get to that point. And I'll continue this trek as long as I'm able. But, should the time come, I need to take stock. With the need to let go. And the need to let God.

Trail Log: Day 96

Taking Stock

Letting God

The 'letting go' bit is tough for me. I know it's not giving up on me. But letting go feels so final. Like the last pages in the book of life. Before the glossary and index pages. The end. But, as I was walking along today, I came to know this: Letting go is hard. It's courageous. It's the right thing to do for me. And I don't need to save it until the very end. I can work on letting go every day. Not just letting go. Like I'm throwing it all to the wind. Checking out. Taking leave. Dropping it off. Dumping it in the corner of the floor.

No. I let go of things in a helpful way when I give it to God to hold and to keep. And to help carry for me. But, in order to do that, I need to also 'let God'. This means that I have to *believe God*, not just believe *in* God. For when I believe in something, I simply hold an opinion or belief about that thing or person. With God, I'm not some distant, third-party bystander. Because I am of God and God is in me, I need to enter into God more. Believe God, not just what I'm told God says or does. Perhaps, when I do that, I can start asking *for* God, instead of asking for lots of stuff from God. You know, taking joy and life from sitting and being with God. Not tiring my arms and my eyes as I wait for all the goodies God is going to bring me. God is not an ATM machine. A goodie bag. A Santa Sack. No. God is beautiful and marvelous and wonderful in God's own right. And that's just what we actually know about God. Wow. What if God is even more amazing than that? Way more.

So, if I believe God and ask for God, I also need to trust God. Not to do what I think is best for me. But to work things out in the end so that God's ends are served. If I truly trust God, I can also trust the ends that God has planned. For me. And everyone else. Even if those ends aren't in my time or in the place I'm in right now. Or want to get to now. I need to let God be God. And to do God's thing. In everlasting love and peace.

Final Thoughts for This Leg

So, I finished another leg of this canyon trail, God. As you know, it's not turned out well. I got bush-wacked. Hit between the eyes. Set back. Turned back. Way back. Some days I seriously doubt that I'll ever get out of here. It's frightening, actually. That I might end up suffering until the end.

And so, I've needed to take stock over the last few days. Stock of 'now what' in the face of it all. Stock of what's still possible for me. I've needed to come to grips. With what hope really means. With what faith demands of me. I've thought about my wishes and my fears a good deal. I've been putting that off for too long—focusing only on the immediate tasks ahead.

Hitting this snag in the trail has slowed me down. And I've taken stock of what's really going on inside of me. Knowing what I aspire to and fear most is cathartic, to be honest. So are the many blessings and losses in my life. I'm glad that I've been sorting these out, as well, of late. I've had a lot of both. I guess that's life. But it's good to take stock of them when I'm feeling down. I've also taken time to reflect on my past. My legacy. What I leave behind for others if I don't get out. I've made a difference along the way. For others. I'm joyful about that, even if I'm not around to see it all.

I have to admit that my feelings about you have taken a hit with this latest setback. But I need only look to the sky and the life around me to know that you have it all covered. I'm part of something bigger than me. You've not forgotten me. But you see me in tune with all living things. I have to trust that. I have to let go sometimes. I have to accept the stuff that I'll never fully understand. To be one with everything. Your entire creation. Your plan. Your vision for this world. Your Reign.

In so doing, I need to let you be God. Not just the God that I understand in my limited ways. But the one who is more amazing and wonderful than anything I could ever imagine. That defies my feeble descriptions. That defies all description. Let me let you do your thing, Lord. I'll be healed in the end, no matter what. I'll be safe and loved and wanted and cared for and gently held. No matter what. I can live with that, God.

Canyon Trail Leg Ten:
What We Need in Caregivers

"Let the favor of the Lord our God be upon us, and prosper for us the work of our hands—O prosper the work of our hands!"

PSALM 90: 17

Leg Ten Canyon Trail Preview

THANK YOU FOR HELPING me to climb those steep hills on the last leg, God. Thank you for helping me to let go and give it to you. Because, frankly, I was shot. You carried me. I know it. And I'm grateful. For just when I thought that all was lost forever, I finally found a way off of the main trail today. You know, off the one that's well marked. . . but taking me backwards on. You know, because the main trail is blocked ahead. Washed out, actually.

This new development makes me hopeful and even happy, Lord. It's far from any guarantee out, to be sure. I have absolutely no idea where this new 'path' will take me. But it's a live option here. Perhaps the only one which can get me out. Alive. That's a live option, I guess. And it looks even more manageable than the main trail. That's a plus. And it's mostly downhill. Plus, plus. Slight, steady downward grade. Less strenuous, by far. Plus, plus, plus. Wow, I'm thinking that I might just make it out of here, after all. Major multiple plus.

But there's one final challenge on this leg: This 'path' is *not* on the map. And there may be lots of 'forks in the road' ahead. Lots of chances to make the right call. Or the wrong call. A bad call means a longer way out. Or no way out. A better call means a shorter way out. A surer way out. And, in order to make the right choices, I need to care for myself. For if I don't care for myself, I may not care at all. About the best way out. Then I'm out. Over. And Out. Major multiple minuses.

God, please help me to love myself enough to care for myself while I'm off the beaten path here. To take care of myself as I encounter the many forks in the road ahead. Because the fork that looks like the best might not actually be the best. Care for me in taking the right fork. The best fork, no matter the barriers, perceived or real. Care for me in choosing your fork. The one that takes me to a place that you want me to go. Even when I'm not sure I want to go. And help me take just one fork at a time. With faith in your faithfulness, Lord. Your direction. Your guidance. Your judgment. Let me give the forks to you. To light the way. To make each fork 'your fork'. For you will make it right no matter which fork. Thanks, in advance, Lord.

Trail Log: Day 97

Barriers to Caring

Systems Based

I FOUND A POSSIBLE way forward today. A path from the main trail. You know, the one I was walking backwards on. This new path appears to take me back in the right direction. I'm hopping mad at myself that I wasn't the least bit curious about this when I passed it before. I guess I got lost in the big picture and all the self-inflicted 'noise' that I had been beating myself with in my effort to get out of this canyon quickly. But, with nothing to lose, I took the new path today.

Along the way, I began to think about all the other stuff that gets in my way. In the way of my helping myself more—and of others helping me. This canyon is fairly simple. Even then, I missed a possible shortcut out. I think about the wider world in which I live. It's messy. It's complicated. It's noisy and loud. It's segmented. It's not joined up at all. Everything seems to be too complex for me. I don't understand the half of it, actually. A bit like drinking water out of a large fire hose with the pressure turned up to high. Hit it! And you have to be a Ph.D. in order to turn the hose on or off. Takes an advanced degree just to regulate the pressure. So we need specialists to design the hose. Specialists to build the hose. Specialists to turn the hose on and off. Specialists to explain the hose to all of us. And, by the way, none of the specialists talk to each other. They each talk to me separately. They're not joined up. As a result, neither am I. Everybody works in silos. Might as well be nuclear silos for all the good they do for me. And for my suffering.

What I need are people who truly care about me. And who speak in *my* language, not some specialist gibberish. And who join up the conversation in ways that it hangs together. Rather than in ways that simply confuse me. I need people who actually talk to me. As a person. In my own language. Not some silo-laden, fractured techno-babble. If you care about me, please sit down with me. Talk with me. Humanly.

Trail Log: Day 98

Barriers to Caring

Individually Based

THE ONE NICE THING about this canyon is its balance. Nature seems to work in balance. In fact, it seems to work just fine whether I'm here or not. It worked before I got here. It'll work long after I'm out of here. It doesn't depend on me to keep the trains running around here. It runs on schedule quite nicely no matter what. Being here has drawn me into this cycle of nature. Being here reminds me that I am part of something bigger. Big. I'm not the biggest thing in the place. I'm not the brightest bulb. I'm not the most beautiful part of the scenery. And that's OK. It's nice not to stand out all the time. OK.

This place also reminds me that my life has been full of busyness. Leading up to my suffering, I ran like a deer. I had checklists. To do lists. Past due lists. Way past due lists. Reminders to check my lists. Post it notes. Sticky notes. Yarn on my finger. Daily readings to keep me going. Weekly quotes to keep me motivated. And the more that I tried to stay on my schedule, the more the interruptions seemed to come. In fact, my life became a raging battle. Like some announcer was saying, "Ladies and Gentlemen. Let's get ready to rumble. In this corner, we have the ever-present and translucent *Busyness*. And in the other, we have the challenger, the ever-awakening and always bothersome *Interruptions*. Go to your corners and come out fighting at the bell. Keep it dirty tonight, gentlemen. Good luck." Yeah.

I think I've used my busyness and the interruptions in my life as an excuse. To avoid my deep and underlying pain. For too long. So. . . I think I need others to help me slow down. To help me to trash the lists for a while. Help me to spend some time with the interruptions. Maybe just maybe, the interruptions are the most important thing. Maybe they're telling me something big about me. Maybe the interruptions contain the seeds of happiness. The seeds of healing. The seeds of me.

Trail Log: Day 99

Barriers to Caring
Ownership Based

I WAS THINKING MORE about the need to slow down as I walked today. It was kind of weird, actually. The more that I thought about slowing down, the slower I walked. Without thinking about physically slowing down. Like my thoughts took ownership of my body without my telling my body to ease up a bit in my trek. Very interesting.

And it got me to wondering this: How much ownership have I actually been taking in this journey of mine? This journey of life. Of suffering. Of pain. Of loss. Of sadness. How many times in my life have I walked by someone in need . . . then kept walking? With nary a thought about it. Nada, really. Because I was busy. Tied up. Tied down.

In truth, I was avoiding the truth that sat before me. Right in front of my face. The person calling out for help. The injustice and wrong being perpetrated. The need going unmet. Sometimes that person, wrong, or need was of someone or something else. But sometimes, it was of me. Either way, I ignored it. I avoided it. I rationalized it away. I told it to "Hit the road, Jack." I asked it to "Get out of my way, Big Guy. Get gone."

To be fair, some of it may have been my fatigue. Sometimes even compassion fatigue. I've tried to help others wherever I can. Others have tried to help me. But none of us ever took care of us along the way. So we burned out. Burned up. To a crisp. Then gave up.

Some of it is due to stress. You're stressed. I'm stressed. Everybody's stressed. Yep. So, we all keep trucking along. Avoiding. Burning out. Stressing out. Freaking out. Until we're totally out. Out of gas. Out of energy. Out of the game of helping others and ourselves. And then, we're out of luck.

Because we need each other to care. To care about us and for us when we're hurting. We need to build up our reserves. Of care. And we need to 'own' caring as our responsibility. Not someone else's. Nope. Ours.

Trail Log: Day 100

Barriers to Caring

Distance Based

THIS CANYON IS ONE huge place. In case you haven't been reading. It's humongous. It seems to go on forever. If I were to yell out at the top of my lungs, no one would hear me anyway. Not outside of a mile or so. And that's just a fraction of the size of the canyon floor. Heck, if I were hiking with others here, I'd tell them to stay together. It's easy to get separated in such a big space. And if we did, look out. Good luck finding each other.

My life before this canyon feels a little like that, I think. I had become separated from my family, my friends, my former work colleagues, my faith colleagues. Everyone's always on the move. To somewhere. From somewhere. Between someplace and someplace else. It's been hard to stay in touch. To stay in communication. To stay in their lives. And them in mine. Staying in human contact is hard, arduous work. And it's a challenge.

But, then again, it's not the only one. It's also hard to stay in touch with other generations. We have our generational labels: Boomers, X-ers, Y-ers, Millennials. These separate us, too. Because they put us in buckets. Pull us apart. Give us our values and our tendencies. As if you can measure us in some precise way. Really? Don't think so.

Lastly, we separate ourselves culturally, linguistically, religiously, and economically. By gender. By sexual preference. By lifestyle. By our politics. By our hobbies. Yuk.

I need people in my life from *all* walks of life. Diverse. I need everyone who cares. I need people who care more about others than where they stand, how much they make, who or how much they know, where they live, which generation they come from, what their ethnicity is, or how old they are. Frankly, when I suffer, I don't give a lick about any of that. It suddenly doesn't matter one whit. Because it shouldn't. For we share one thing in common: Our human heart. This heart was made to care for us and each other. To keep beating with love.

Trail Log: Day 101

Barriers to Caring
Worldview Based

THE MORE I GOT to thinking about my trail guide map, the madder I became today. Why didn't the map contain this alternate route that I'm now on? At least as a backup plan if the trail ahead got washed out. Like it actually did. Why was the main path out the 'only' path? When, in fact, it wasn't actually. For I'm now on another path. Maybe out of here. But I have no way of knowing for sure. Because the guide map doesn't tell me about it.

The folks making this map had a bad case of tunnel vision. Or the people gave up and created some trails for themselves. Different ones. Perhaps better ones. But the trail map crowd wouldn't hear of it. So they censured the other views. To my detriment, for sure.

When I slowly calmed myself down today, I reflected on my own life and suffering. And I had to admit that my life has been a lot like the trail map. I've formed my opinions along the way. My worldview of sorts. Which is good, actually. To stand for something. To value something. To believe in something.

All good. . . until I try to impose this 'something' on everyone else in the room. Or superimpose my own feelings onto those of others. Like when I tell my fellow-sufferers, "I understand what you're going through. I had something just like it two years ago. Don't worry. I made it. So will you." And in so doing, I quit caring and started preaching. Then I stopped preaching and started meddling. Then I started imposing.

In the end, I'm entitled to my experiences, survival stories, pity-parties, suffering, and sad endings. But they're mine. Not the other guy's. He or she has a suffering unique to him or her. They are not me. And I am not them. While my experiences might be similar, theirs are unique to them. What I need are people who will simply shut up sometimes. And just sit with me. I need to do that with others a whole lot more, as well. When they suffer their own pains. Theirs uniquely. Not mine.

Trail Log: Day 102

The Role of the Caregiver

I MADE SOME REAL headway on the new path today. Actually, amazing headway to be clear. In only a few days, I've made it past the washed-out streambed. The one that sent me backwards a few weeks back. Now I'm faced with a dilemma, though. Do I get back on the main trail or stay with the less beaten one that I'm now on. I have a lot to lose by making the wrong choice here. The main path will most certainly get me out in the end. But there are more streambeds ahead. The less traveled path appears dryer, flatter, and more direct. But it comes with some risk. I don't know if it will get me out of here in the end.

I sat for a while and pondered things. Then decided to stay on the new, unmarked path that I'm now on. I'm going with it, knowing that I can always backtrack again if I need to. And re-catch the main trail out. But I'm hoping that I won't need to. In making this decision today, I had to think about all the factors involved here. There are many. I had to call into play many parts of me in order to do the best thing for me.

And doing so reminds me that I need to care for me more holistically going forward. Being a better caregiver for me is being lots of things for me: Pastor. Counselor. Social Worker. Comforter. Confidant. Facilitator. Connector. Friend. Companion. Helper. Sitter. Chaplain. All those things. All of them. Perhaps not all at once. But all of them to some degree or another. At one point or another. On the journey of my suffering, pain, and loss. I don't need advanced degrees to be these things. To me or to others who suffer.

I *do* need to know the limits of what I know. I need not get in over my head. And I have to be able to admit to myself when I'm starting to get there. The over my head part. Then help myself or others find the right people who *can* help. In a more knowledgeable way. You know, get out of the way, while staying there beside the way. That's the way.

Trail Log: Day 103

What the Role Implies

So, I've decided to stay on the 'other' path. The unmarked one. I'm going for it anyway. Even though it's far from guaranteed. But I've decided that caring for myself in this place has to mean something. Something other than the 'standard' way. Something different than the same path that everyone else always takes: The wide, 'safe', and nicely paved road.

Caring for me and for others *differently* means that I have to be 'on the ground'. Boots on the ground. Mine. Actually, not boots. Boots need some feet to make them walk. Those feet are mine. This new, unmarked path is closer to the ground than the other. The main trail tends to wind above the canyon floor. Follows the rock walls around various passes. Nice views, but a lot of ups and downs. I feel more a part of the canyon on *this* new path. I need to keep my boots firmly planted in the soil. Doing so entails some risk to be sure. This path may take me nowhere. Or could even be a loop. Back to where I picked it up days ago. But it appears to be headed the right way. So I'm taking the risk. A good risk. Taking this risk is actually being good to myself here. It is less strenuous, more peaceful. And it might get me out of here faster, as it turns out.

I need to keep open to more things like this path. Which help me to care for myself and for others. Better self-care also means that I have to become far more self-aware. As I reflect, I realize that I need to look beyond the surface wounds of my canyon walk. Beyond the cuts and scrapes and bruises and blisters and sunburn and tired feet. I must look courageously inside of me, as well. It's the stuff below the surface that really counts. The stuff that eats me alive, if I'm honest. So, I need to pay more attention to that inside stuff. And I need to do a better job of helping others do that, too. When I get out of here. There, I said it. "*When*. Not if."

Trail Log: Day 104

Into the Chaos

God

YEAH, I ACTUALLY SAID it again today. "*When* I finally walk out of this canyon." It felt good to hear that. First I said it silently. In my head. In my heart. In my soul. Then I said it out loud. Softly. Louder. Louder yet. Then I yelled it out. Really loudly. So loud that the sounds of my cry came back to me in the ringing echoes of the canyon walls. I liked hearing it coming back to me. So I yelled it out again. Then I smiled. At first, I hesitated to let the feeling last. Hard to trust hope and optimism. When I've felt so bad for so long. When I came so close to getting stuck in here forever. Or dying in here. Now that's forever. And ever. It was chaotic. It felt chaotic. Completely.

But God entered into the chaos. God is bigger than chaos. The nature of chaos is its temporality. God is permanent. Chaos can't compete. Perhaps I can't either. Getting out of this canyon won't fix all my problems. Some parts may heal. Other parts may never heal. At least as others have defined the word 'heal'. And I will not live forever on this earth. But God is here amidst the chaos of it all. God has brought calmness, compassion, communion, connection, creativity, new insights, and a wholeness that I've never felt before in my life. Who would have thought it? That this journey in the canyon brought something other than greater misery. It did. Because God did. God was fully present with me. Making 'me' important to God's own very self.

To be sure, God confronted me with 'myself', my beliefs, my values, my purpose, and my mission. God started the hard conversations with me that I didn't want to really have at all. Sometimes, the dialogue stung. Made me uneasy. Uncomfortable. But I never had to do it alone. I may still have a little ways yet to go out of this canyon, but I thank God for it. For God has taken this place. And God has made something out of nothing. That's something. That's really something, God. Thanks!

Final Thoughts for This Leg

I THINK I'VE FOUND the best way out of here, God. The scrubby, unmarked trail may have been the best path after all. Who would have thought it? I sure didn't. Getting close to the end has me looking back. At how I've cared for me and for others. In my own suffering. And that of others. It's not been a pretty sight, if I'm honest. So many things get in the way of caring. The whole system feels rigged. Like the very forces that are here to help me actually hurt me.

I've been my own worst enemy, too, though. I've gotten in my own way along the way. I've failed to 'own' my care, my feelings, my actions, and my future. I've put distance between me and me. I've distanced myself from others. Even those who are hurting. Because it all makes me feel uncomfortable. And I've let my own beliefs and opinions block the way to others. It's been more important to be right than to do right by others. In other words, Lord, I've done a poor job of caring for me, for those who want to help me, and for those who hurt alongside me. I don't judge me for it. But I need to change because of what I've learned.

I ask that you help me to be a better caregiver, God. It's not rocket-science. I don't need an advanced degree. Or a certificate. Or a genius IQ. I need to be careful not to overstep the bounds of care. To know when I'm in over my head. But I can do so much for myself and for others who also hurt. And it starts by getting my feet on the ground of my suffering.

Help me to actually 'land' in the canyon of suffering. Not just a fly-by. Help me to be truly present for others. Even when others don't ask for me. For *you're* asking for me, Lord. Right now. You have entered into the chaos of this canyon. The chaos of my suffering and pain. The chaos of my losses. And you've helped me to make some sense of it all. Not all of it all. But a start to it all. And that's all I can ask. Amen.

Final Thoughts from the Trail

Today, I reached the end of the canyon. I did it! I actually made it! Finally. And I was just about to step out of it. Relieved. Done. Out of here. But here's the thing. As I was about to exit, I felt this voice inside of me. The voice was soft. Almost a whisper. But I could hear it clearly. Perhaps more clearly than I've ever heard anyone before. The voice said, "Take off your glasses." To be honest, I don't wear glasses. At least I don't recall ever wearing them at any point during my canyon trek these past months. But maybe I was. . . and who was I to argue with this voice? So, I removed my glasses. Then the voice asked me to look around. And I did.

Without my glasses, I now looked upwards. I saw the simple, plain lines of the horizon. Beautiful, actually. Broad and expansive. Enormous. Not the narrow, closed-in view that I'd had before. Then I looked more closely at the canyon walls. And I saw the many colored contours on them. The varied shapes. The wonder of their formations. Not the plain, enclosing walls that I'd seen before. Then I looked down. I saw the growth around me. The plants. The living things. Their joyful, playful movement. The color and splendor of something so simple, yet so grand. Not the plain, brown sand and dust I'd seen before. Then I looked to the sky. I saw brilliant blue, dotted with billowy white clouds. This time, they literally danced and leapt across the sky. I no longer saw the grey fog and mist that I'd seen on some days before. I saw the canyon all around me. But it was different. Way different. Without the glasses.

The voice asked me what I made of all of this. I was struck by the very absence of my initial response. But after a few moments, I asked the voice, "Where is the canyon? The canyon of my suffering? The canyon of my imprisonment? The one that I've tried so hard to navigate and exit from for the past few months?" And the voice returned, "The lens with which you viewed your suffering colored your vision. It closed you in. It cut you off. It shut you down. And with this lens, you turned the canyon into a place of further suffering. A prison. A place largely *of your own* making."

The voice continued. It said, "You are now ready to exit this place. Are you sure that you truly want this? With the new lens I've now given you? The lens and view without the glasses that you were wearing before. For, while you made this canyon a dungeon, you also survived. You lived. You learned. You felt. You expressed. You cried out to me. I heard you all along. I helped you walk. I gave you breath. I inspired your mind, your thoughts, and your very soul. And *you* are now different as a result. You are transformed. Not out of your suffering, but within it."

I reflected and asked, "What must I now do to experience the *real* canyon? The one that I didn't fully see before. I want to go there now." And the voice replied, "You will *always* be there if you seek me. If you seek to know me. And to better know yourself and others in that process. For this is the only way." The voice then asked me to pick up the book beside me. I opened the book to this:

> "How precious is your steadfast love, O God! All people may take refuge in the shadow of your wings. They feast on the abundance of your house, and you give them drink from the river of your delights. For with you is the fountain of life; in your light we see light."
> —Psalms 36: 7–9

With that, I simply sat and reflected. I was refreshed. I was at peace. I looked out beyond the end of the canyon. Beyond the exit. I looked again. And then I closed my eyes and looked inside myself. Deeply. I looked inside my heart. Even more deeply. Then I turned around. I looked behind me at the canyon with my new lens. With my transformed eyes without the glasses. I looked back upon the place I'd walked before those many days. Yet didn't fully know. And I walked back in. Right back into the canyon. Retracing new steps home.

Things That I Need to Think Even More About

About Me

WHO AND WHAT HAVE I become in my own suffering? If I'm honest, what am I actually feeling right now (specifically named) about my suffering and why?

In the midst of my pain and loss, what am I most afraid of and why? What are my most guarded and unspoken fears, needs, assumptions, and secrets that need to be surfaced and safely dealt with in my life right now?

How have I become imprisoned by my suffering, anger, and hurt? How have I been most victimized by all that has happened to me? How much have I allowed *myself* to become a 'victim' as a result? How can I more fully empower myself going forward?

What do I most need to come to terms with if I don't fully heal in my suffering? What things must I take stock of that can help me to move forward along the uncertain path ahead?

About God

How have I actually experienced God in the midst of my suffering? What has most influenced me in this regard? How helpful is my current 'picture' of God in my efforts to heal?

How do I define God's power, goodness, and justice in a world where suffering exists? How do I actually approach God with my needs when I suffer? Do I want God. . . or do I want God to simply *do something* to make my suffering go away?

About My Behaviors

What things am I doing that actually prolong or worsen my suffering? How am I most getting in the way of myself as I try to heal?

How have my own past history and 'story' about myself impacted my view of myself, my current behaviors, and my perceptions about my suffering?

How has the pain that I've tried so hard to cover-up and paper-over continued to create new or exacerbated suffering for me right now?

About My Relationships

How are other people or things acting on my suffering in ways that help or hurt me? What boundaries can I create or better manage in order to influence things in a more positive direction in my life— where I can actually make a difference?

How have I become most 'disconnected' in my life as a result of my suffering? Who or what can I better reconnect with in order to help me heal? What do I need to do more of or less of in order to make greater connectivity possible?

How caring and empathetic toward myself and toward others am I really? What gets in the way and why? How can I address the biggest barriers here in an effort to become a better and more loving caregiver? How would becoming more caring help me and help others for whom I care?

About My Spirituality

How do I define being 'Spiritual' in my life right now? How has my suffering changed this view and why? What practices can I adopt to achieve greater, healthier, more supportive, and healing Spirituality for me in the future?

How can I become more at-peace, integrated, and whole in the midst of ongoing movement, fluidity, randomness, and change? How can even my suffering create some transformation, meaning, and purpose in my life and in my faith right now?

Postscript

As Spiritual people of belief and faith, it is easy to feel that we are called to help others in need. To come alongside those who are poor, mournful, meek, seeking peace, and persecuted. To shine a light on justice, peace, comfort, support, and mercy for them. To help them out. To show them the way. But this might miss the point completely. What if those people whom we try to help already *have* the qualities that God is seeking for the Reign of God? These qualities are already in them. Jesus was asking us to become far more like these folks. Like the meek and humble and poor and those of peace. Because these are the very things that matter in the end. The things that make us human beings in God's image and likeness.

As a hospital chaplain, I am often asked to pray for patients and their families. In the midst of life's most terrible trials, sickness, loss and sorrow, suffering, pain, hopelessness and sadness, and fear. I have been asked for words of comfort, encouragement, wisdom, praise, and insight. And, while I typically do far more listening than speaking, I *do* offer these prayers and words along the way. But I've also learned this along the way: The greatest words, prayers, gifts, insights, sources of inspiration, and thanks have never come from me. Nor from the mouths of other chaplains or pastors or priests. For, however hard we try, the power to heal comes most often from within the very hearts of those who suffer. Fueled by God and by their own Spirituality. Visited by the Spirit, perhaps. Harnessed by whatever source of transcendence that they find meaningful. But from within themselves, nonetheless.

The greatest prayer I've ever heard came not from my mouth. It was from a patient in a hospital where I served. The patient prayed in simple, direct terms. It was almost childlike. Pure. Thoughtful. Innocent. Thankful. Trusting. It was simply beautiful. Following the patient's prayer, she asked me to pray. I did so, but I felt very small in doing so. I told the patient that whatever I might now say paled in comparison to the sheer might, splendor, and wisdom of her own words. And then I feebly spoke to God. I reminded God that God had just heard the wisest, most incredible words that I may have ever heard. I asked God to truly hear *her*. Why would I want to spoil her words with mine?

The greatest wisdom that I've ever heard was not from teachers or professors or doctors or nurses or social workers or even other chaplains. I've learned far more from the patients themselves. I visited one patient who told me that his own 'canyon' of suffering was one that he'd built himself. He had laid the foundations and the walls. He had created the dry, dusty ground. He had created the biting, cold winds. He had hidden the sun within a thick layer of fog and mist. He had gotten lost because he stopped trying to find a way within it all. The patient told me it was only in getting older, in facing his own pending mortality, that he could truly find the gift of knowing what was most important in the end. That it is only by embracing the vast mysteries of God, and the many questions posed by these mysteries, that he could find ultimate truth. The patient told me it was only by his becoming a burden to others that he could see the importance of carrying the burdens of others each day. That only in letting go of things could he truly acquire the things that he needed most at this time in his life. Finally, he told me it was only in his sorrows, losses, and limitations that he was now able to know true freedom, joy, and laughter.

The greatest blessing I've ever received as a chaplain is not a plaque. Not a certificate. Not a book. Not a good review. Not a paycheck. Not even close. The greatest gift was a hug from grieving families as I later left the hospital room of their now-passed relatives. A gift of thanks for coming. For sitting with them. For simply being there. For sometimes offering words of comfort, Scripture, and prayer. But mostly for taking the time to care. What a gift. And from people who somehow found a way to say 'thank you' on the worst day of their lives.

The greatest 'thanks' that I've ever received was from a homeless patient who was leaving the hospital after an extended stay. We had spent a number of visits together. The patient's face was beaming as she prepared to depart. She could hardly contain her smile. She turned to me and said, "Thank you for everything, chaplain. I won't forget." And as she spoke, she turned to leave. Everything she owned was packed tightly onto a baby stroller that she wheeled from the hospital. This *was* her home. And I felt thanked in a profound, nearly indescribable way that day. Humbled by the resilient spirit of another human being.

The greatest courage I've ever seen is *not* that of the doctors and nurses who tend to patients. Theirs is courageous work, to be sure. I have witnessed the steely focus, the enormous talent, the intellect, and the insights of those who clinically heal patients in the most tenuous of situations. In the Emergency Department. In the Trauma Bay. In Intensive Care. In the Psychiatric Unit. In Physical Rehab units. Everywhere, actually. High stakes places. Lots of courage needed. In the moment. Over the long haul. But theirs are not the greatest examples. No. The greatest courage I've ever seen is from our veterans, our warriors, who have now returned from overseas. Who fought the wars for us.

Postscript

And who now come home scarred. Who don't believe that we can ever understand them. What they've gone through. Who they've lost over there. The lives they've had to take. The trauma of it all. The Post Traumatic Stress Syndrome that they now face. The flashbacks. The nightmares. They tell me they have literally 'lost their very souls'. But they somehow continue on. And seek peace and healing. Because they are warriors at heart. Their courage eclipses anything that I've ever seen before.

The greatest gift that I've ever given a patient is not a prayer. Not a Bible. Not a devotional. Not a word of encouragement, comfort, solace, or anything even remotely like that. No. My greatest chaplain gift to a patient was a simple card. A business card. It was for our Pastoral Services team. It had the usual contact stuff on it. What made it so special, though, was what it *didn't* have on it. It didn't have my name embossed. I had just spent nearly an hour with an elderly patient who was being discharged momentarily. She was despondent, desperately lonely, and overwhelmed. I had visited with her some days before. When I entered the room on this day, she remembered my name. She said to me, "You're Jeff Tucker, the chaplain." I was frankly shocked. She had met people by the busload while staying as an inpatient at the hospital. Nurses and doctors. Specialists. Generalists. Social Workers. Tech staff. Nutritional staff. All kinds of folks. And yet she remembered my name. She had so many other things to deal with, including her own trepidation about going home to her nursing facility to die. And yet she remembered my name. After our visit on her last day at the hospital, we prayed together. She cried throughout most of my prayer. I felt terribly inadequate that day. As if I should have done something more for her. To give her something important and profound to hold onto. In my feeble attempt to do something, I pulled out a pastoral services card. And I wrote my name on it with a pen. I gave it to the patient and told her this: "When you feel lonely in the days and weeks ahead, please pull this card out. And remember that someone cares about you. The person you remembered by name. You have a name, too. A special one. That I'll remember. Neither of us will be alone. We can pray for each other by name." Later that day, I was feeling guilty about the card. How cold. How impersonal. But, as I reflected on it more in the days ahead, I realized that the blank business card was exactly the best thing to give her. Because I had made it mine. With my name. For her. And only her. Personalized. I thank God for giving me the courage to do something so small, so risky, and yet so profoundly caring and personal for her.

The greatest things that I've ever received or have given in my pastoral work came from the hearts of the patients, themselves. I have looked into the blank, numbed faces of those who were abused as children or as adults. I have looked into the wounded hearts of those who grew up amidst drug and alcohol dependence or abuse in their families of origin. I have searched the hearts of those who lost their soul fighting bloody wars in foreign lands. I have sat with those who have lost their children, parents, family, friends, and even perfect strangers in cases of sudden, traumatic deaths. I have shared the concurrent joy, sorrow, memories, grief, and confusion as family members have stood bedside with a dying loved one when aggressive life support is withdrawn. I have held the promise of my accompaniment and hope to those who find no reason to go on or to live another day. I have befriended those whose only present and reliable friend has been a bottle of vodka. I have listened to those with only days to live as they come to terms with their fears, hopes, legacies, losses, regrets, and their proudest moments. I have tried to hear those who suffer. To listen very hard. Not just to their story and their words, but to their feelings, their affect, and their very souls. Those things may be unspoken, but are deeply moving within them.

The truest beauty, the truest answers, the truest insights, and the truest gifts belong to those who suffer. They come not from bookshelves or the countless stacks in a seminary library. They do not come from the pulpit at church. They don't come from a lectern in a lecture hall. Not from a journal. Not from the sage wisdom of a noted philosopher. Not from those wearing a collar or the sacred garments of a priest or pastor. No. They come from those who wear faded hospital gowns. Who live in the streets. Who face sudden or chronic illnesses. Who face the sunset years of their lives. Who now face their very mortality. Who have seemingly lost all power to control. Who see their very finiteness and limits in stark, real, and darkly vivid terms. Who have every reason to give up, to pull away, to close down, to shut out, or to close out. But they do not. These people have faced their suffering. They have looked at this suffering squarely in the eye. And they didn't blink. Because they decided to let God in. To let God work in it, not outside of it. To let God ruminate within their bodies and within their souls. To let God be God. To let God draw nearer in the process. And, in turn, to restore their souls: Their very God-given, innate capacity and responsibility for fullness and integration as unconditionally loved human beings. As God works, God restores hope. This hope rises within us. Resurrects us from within us. From the ashes of despair. From the pits of fear. From the abyss of suffering, pain, loss, and even death. Yes, even death. For God is bigger than death. And God will never leave us here or even there. No matter what. There is always hope. No matter what.

With Infinite Gratitude

MUCH OF THE INSPIRATION for this book comes from my time as a Chaplain Resident with a Philadelphia area hospital. A significant portion of our work as Residents centers on our pastoral work within the hospital units themselves. We visit myriad patients one-on-one throughout each day. We staff the Emergency Department, supporting patients, families, and staff in cases of stroke, heart attacks, emergency resuscitations, and traumas. We attend family meetings to support decision-making for chronically or emergently ill patients. We participate in debriefs of patient contact and care situations to ensure ongoing quality and responsiveness. We do all those things, to be sure. But we also learn together. We learn about our work as chaplains. About the skills and behaviors that make us better at what we do. In order to serve our patients, their families, and our staff. We learn from books, verbatims, articles, role-plays, and the like. But we learn, as well, from informal sharing. Sharing our experiences, feelings, insights, ideas, fears, and hopes. I, therefore, thank my chaplain residency colleagues for the opportunity to learn with them. And to share this precious time with them all along the way. All this would not be possible without the support and guidance of Clinical Pastoral Supervisors such as Stephen Dutton, Metty Messick, and Linda Grant. I am very grateful to each of them, as well for helping to guide and shape my work.

Also, I thank one of my many seminary professors in particular: Dr. Loida Martell-Otero for her role in my theological formation. She, more than any other teacher, helped to form how I think theologically. She inspired me to push the boundaries of theology responsibly and thoughtfully. She helped me to think contextually. She gave voice, in my thinking, to the voices that this world too often forgets to hear: Those of the poor, marginalized, forgotten, sick, and powerless. I am the chaplain that I am today, in part, because of Dr. Martell.

Lastly, I thank my family. I thank my two grown children, Ashley and Zachary, for their continued encouragement, their support, their modeled courage in the face of their own respective setbacks in life, their resiliency, and the power of their loving spirits. And I thank my wife, Carmen. Next to God, she is the beaming light and love in my life. She has given me the space, the freedom, and the blessing to write not just one book, but now a second one. At times, she has sacrificed my time with her for the focus that I've needed to have in writing this new book. She has continued to encourage me to write. She has encouraged me to find my voice. And she has encouraged me to add a new voice to those of many others who speak on behalf of those who suffer. I would be far poorer for not having walked with her each and every day throughout the entirety of our adult lives. I thank God that I did not have to. Next to God, I thank God for Carmen most of all.

www.ingramcontent.com/pod-product-compliance
Lightning Source LLC
Chambersburg PA
CBHW051933160426
43198CB00012B/2132